The Ultimate Evidence

The Ultimate Evidence

Rethinking the Evidence
Issues for Spirit-baptism

LARRY VERN NEWMAN

WIPF & STOCK · Eugene, Oregon

THE ULTIMATE EVIDENCE
Rethinking the Evidence Issues for Spirit-baptism

Wipf & Stock
A Division of Wipf and Stock Publishers
199 W. 8th Ave., Suite 3
Eugene, OR 97401
www.wipfandstock.com

ISBN 13: 978-1-4982-5201-0

To
Donald G. Bloesch,
teacher, mentor, friend

Contents

Abbreviations

A/G	Assemblies of God
CGCT	Church of God (Cleveland, TN)

Foreword

THE WORK OF THE Holy Spirit is a debated area in the church world today. Will a new book on the Holy Spirit further muddy the waters? The church certainly does not need greater confusion as she endeavors to minister in our present world. Dr. Newman's writing intends to clear the waters. I believe the strength of his work is his identification of the *primary* purpose and *continuing* evidence of a Spirit-filled community. The church must be certain of the power that binds her together and equips and enables her for effective witness to the person and work of Jesus Christ.

Newman offers more than a personal opinion. He proposes a proper hermeneutical model founded upon basic principles introduced by some of the great interpreters and theologians of the Christian faith, particularly Karl Barth. If it is granted that we must consult Barth on Christology, should we bypass him relative to Pnuematology? Newman shows how Barth guides us in this area. Hermeneutics must be the groundswell for inquiry as theologians continue their approach to the work of the Holy Spirit.

Dr. Newman is well aware of the controversy among Pentecostals which may result from this work. I do not expect that we will agree with all his conclusions. What I do expect (and this will prove the value of his study) is that many responders will *clear the waters* even further as they build on the issues Dr. Newman raises. This will strengthen the church, and this is precisely Dr. Newman's hope and desire.

Let us, then, welcome this work, examine it thoroughly and thoughtfully, and then respond to it in a manner that honors our witness to Jesus Christ. We must be concerned, above all else, with the edifying of the Body of Messiah through peace and love. And as the global door stands before each of us, we will fulfill the purpose for the coming of the Holy Spirit.

Bruce Arnold Tucker, Ph.D.
Church of God, Cleveland, TN
Acworth, Georgia

Acknowledgments

T HE PREACHER, IN ECCLESIASTES, has stated that there is nothing new under the sun. *Of course, he is right. No one who works with the processing of knowledge can ever be far from the recognition of that truth.*

Since this is true, it is my desire to acknowledge the thousands of Christian scholars and believers who have laid the foundation of knowledge and faith upon which we present day Christians continue to build. This includes both Catholic and Protestant scholars and believers. I stand indebted to them all.

I also express my gratitude to my parents, Winfred V. Newman (dc. 1971) and Ethel Morgan-Newman Kimball (dc. 2000), who left their Methodist heritage to embrace the Pentecostal way; parents who instilled their faith in the hearts of their children and did not waver at the promises of God. They too have a part in this work.

Appreciation must be expressed, as well, to that Christian community into which I was born and received initial nourishment through dedicated Sunday School teachers and youth workers at First Assembly of God, Wenatchee, Washington, for they too are contributors to this monograph.

I must not forget those who have discipled me in the faith. Dear Grandma Downs and Mark Sullivan taught me as a boy. During my time as a student at Northwest University, Professors Daniel B. Pecota and Donald Fee added to my faith and knowledge. Donald G. Bloesch exerted a profound influence upon my life during my years at the University of Dubuque Theological Seminary. Ray S. Anderson, Russell Spittler, Newton Mahoney, and David C. K. Watson impacted my life during my doctoral studies at Fuller Theological Seminary. All of these people have influenced the content of this work.

My wife, Marlena, has an integral part in this work. My special thanks to her for reading the manuscript and doing other preparatory tasks.

My children, Rilla, Michael, Karl, Kurt, Scott, and Karen have all increased my knowledge and brought growth to my faith through the beauty and uniqueness of their persons, as they have endeavored to walk with God. My special thanks to Rilla and Karl, authors in their own right, who have read the manuscript and suggested many pertinent changes. I also express my gratitude to Rilla for help in obtaining sources on the Hellenistic religions from the University of Iowa library.

I wish, as well, to express my appreciation to my friend and colleague, John Rose, who as librarian at Open Bible College was a fine friend and an invaluable aid in locating resources for this work.

Though I acknowledge my indebtedness to all mentioned above, I alone am responsible for the content of this book and I in no way intend to implicate them in its conclusions. However, I am pleased and grateful that they have all touched my life, added to it, and enhanced its quality by doing so!

Finally, I am grateful to the folks at Wipf and Stock Publishers for their quality work in producing this book.

Wenatchee, Washington
August 2008

Introduction

IT IS QUITE AN assertion to claim that one is filled with the Spirit of God. What does a person offer as proof that this is actually true? Pentecostals, at the turn of the twentieth century, proposed an evidence that they thought the scriptures indicated was the primary verification of Spirit-baptism. Many Pentecostals embraced the conclusive notion, but there were also many who did not. It was determined that the evidence to prove that one had been subject to Spirit-baptism was that the person had experienced the exercise of *glossolalia*–they had spoken in an unknown language as prompted by the Holy Spirit. The primary evidence of Spirit-baptism, it was concluded, was the expression of a *charism*; it was charismatic.

Given the fact that people who have laid claim to being Spirit-filled yet have demonstrated a diminished state of character through moral failure, it is right and proper to ask the question, "Is this an adequate evidence that a person has been baptized with the Holy Spirit?" Is there a biblical evidence that has built into its structure strong safeguards that are rock solid, consistent, and easily verifiable? Evidence from a source that is impeccable and unimpeachable, able to stand strong and certain in the highest courts on earth or in heaven or across the breakfast table or over the back fence? Can an evidence be found that is centered, not on what a person does (talk in tongues), but on what a person is (how life is lived)? One that is not charismatic? An evidence that is ethical in substance?

The intent of this work is to rethink the evidential constructs we present day Pentecostals have inherited, with the hope that this will serve as a catalytic source for further dialogue as the theological task goes forward. There are some who think that the issue of tongues-as-evidence ought to be left alone. Then there are some who recognize that the examination and reformation of this doctrine may well be the most important theological endeavor in the history of the Pentecostal movement. Let this be an invitation to engage in this task of rethinking the evidential issues of Spirit-baptism.

THE GOVERNING ABSOLUTE

One dictum governing the theological task must be consistently held before us. That dictum is this: there is one absolute in the theological process that necessarily is the catalytic point of any theological deliberation, and that absolute is *the Word of God*. This principle has been recognized and honored by the guardians of the gospel since the days of the Reformers and must be honored in our day as well.

The church faces grave danger exactly at that point where theological constructs are considered to be absolutes. In other words, our theology must always be open to adjustment or reformation when it is exposed to and judged by a fuller and more competent understanding of the Word of God. Bernard Ramm is correct in his observation relative to theology: "Even though it is in service of the Word of God, in the service of the serious business of preaching, and in the service of the most important of all subject matters, it is nevertheless a very human task that must be done over and over again."[1]

T. F. Torrance has so aptly expressed this truth:

> By its very nature the self-revelation of this God summons us to acknowledge the absolute priority of God's Word over all the media of its communication and reception, and over all understanding and interpretation of its Truth. The Word and Truth of God reach us and address us on their own free ground and on their own authority, for they cannot be understood, interpreted, far less assessed for what they are, on any other standard besides themselves. Hence in all our response to God's Word and in all formula we are summoned to let God retain his own reality, majesty, and authority over against us.[2]

Torrance further avers:

> In divine revelation we have to do with a Word of God which is what it is as a Word of God in its own reality independent of our recognition of it, and we have to do with a Truth of God which is what it is as Truth of God before we come to know it to be true.

---

1. Ramm, *After Fundamentalism*, 194.
2. Torrance, *Evangelical Theology*, 13.

That means that in all our response to God's self-revelation as it is mediated to us in space and time through the Holy Scriptures we must seek to understand and interpret it in accordance with its intrinsic requirements and under the constraint of the truth which bears upon our minds in and through it, and not in accordance with requirements of thought which we bring to it or under the constraint of rigid habits of belief which we retain at the back of our minds irrespective of what we experience beyond ourselves. Divine revelation which commands a response of this kind is very disturbing, for it uproots us from the comfortable certainty of our preconceptions and calls in question the mechanisms we constantly develop in order to give a firmness to our evangelical beliefs in themselves as beliefs, rather than in the objective ground to which as beliefs they are properly correlated and in reference to which they are always open to revision.[3]

A MATURING PEOPLE

Much water has passed under our Pentecostal bridge since the evidential constructs we have inherited were formulated. Great advances have been made in both biblical and theological scholarship. Archeological discoveries have enhanced our knowledge of ancient times and practices. Many of these discoveries have affirmed the validity of the Bible as the Word of God.

The constituency of the classical Pentecostal movement has evolved from a people who were predominantly from the poorer classes to become (through what Donald McGavran has called *lift*) members of America's middle classes.

Classical Pentecostals have become an educated and affluent people. Among our ranks we find the children of those who worshiped in storefronts and canvas tents, who knelt on rough wooden floors or walked sawdust trails, who earned their bread as blue collar workers, people who are the inheritors of their parents' faith but not their poverty or their lack of education. Within our memberships there are those holding advanced degrees from various disciplines, such as attorneys, medical doctors, teachers, businessmen, engineers, and college professors. In ever increasing numbers the pastors and denominational leaders of most Pentecostal

---

3. Ibid., 13–14.

bodies are earning advanced degrees from our nation's universities and seminaries.

The Assemblies of God and the Church of God (Cleveland, TN), two of the largest Pentecostal denominations, have established, accredited theological seminaries. Fuller Theological Seminary in Pasadena, California, has Pentecostals on its faculty. Gordon-Conwell Theological Seminary's former president, Robert Cooley, was a Pentecostal. In addition Regent College in Vancouver, British Columbia, and Southwest Missouri State University in Springfield, Missouri, to name a few, have Pentecostals on their faculties.

Many of the Pentecostal movement's Bible Colleges have evolved to become universities. For example, Northwest College of the Assemblies of God, Kirkland, WA, which began as Northwest Bible Institute in 1934, became Northwest University in 2006. It is comprised of six schools: Arts & Sciences, Ministry, Education, Nursing, Business, and Graduate Psychology. All of this takes place on a beautiful fifty-six-acre modern campus. It is a long stretch from Bible institute to university, and a great deal of "rethinking" was required to get there. Many students were not enrolling in ministry studies; they were attending state and private universities. Leadership persons concluded that there is more to ministry and mission than just training pastors and missionaries. Under the school leadership a new *Field of Dreams*-like vision of Northwest was born. *If you build it they will come.* Responding to the ramped-up curriculum, new facilities, and a new motto, "Carry the Call," new generations of Pentecostal students are answering the call to become people of commerce, healthcare professionals, educators, and so forth. The point is that there had to be a willingness to question the adequacy of the existing purpose and mission of the school as it faced a new era.

What has just been described is a people in the process of maturing. An important aspect of that maturing process has been, and will continue to be, our struggle with the ongoing theological task. As a people, we have reformed our theology relative to many issues. Granted, to this point some issues have been peripheral, but we have demonstrated a willingness to rethink our position on many matters and have made needed adjustments, such as the rejection of our former legalistic concepts regarding the use of cosmetics, women's dress codes, and participation in sports.

A TIME TO CONSOLIDATE AND ADVANCE?

I sincerely believe that the time has come to rethink our protected areas, which we call our *Pentecostal distinctives*. William MacDonald, a Pentecostal, has pointed to the need for new direction in Pentecostal thought:

> Certainly it is no discredit to our spiritual forefathers in this century if they confined themselves primarily to the vehicles of popular written communication (e.g., tracts, magazines and sermon books). These were the generations of change and revival, and the literature was appropriate to the cause. Now the success of the Pentecostal revival calls for consolidation and advance, for continuous searching of the Scripture, careful scholarship, competent sifting of the oral tradition, and comparative study with other Christian traditions.[4]

In the same vein, MacDonald further observes:

> It would be a mistake to assume that in the last seven decades Pentecostal theology has been developed to its limits. On the contrary only certain basics have taken theological form. Foremost among these stands the doctrine that the filling with the Spirit is invariably accompanied by speaking in other languages under the Spirit's control. Though two influential European Pentecostal pioneers, T.B. Barratt and George Jeffreys, did not hold to this tenet, it has maintained a general preponderance of acceptance over the years by classical Pentecostals, and it appears to be no less entrenched in Neo Pentecostal theology. This central belief remains open for further clarification and certification as does any doctrine . . . for the tradition must always be open to biblical correctives.[5]

However, there seems to be a reluctance to reassess doctrine considered unique, thus imposing upon these doctrinal positions an *absoluteness* with which they must not be invested. Subjecting other aspects of our *Pentecostal faith* to a fresh scrutiny by the Word of God, in the light of advanced evangelical scholarship and archeological discoveries, has helped us to a fuller and more competent understanding of the written Word. In the same way, we must also surrender doctrines that are distinct to Pentecostalism to that same scrutiny.

---

4. MacDonald, "Pentecostal Theology," 59–60.

5. Ibid., 68–73.

Roy Blizzard, an archeologist and Hebrew Studies scholar, has observed:

> As a result of the archeological discoveries and the textual studies of the past 35 years, we are now able to understand the Bible, and especially the words of Jesus, as never before in the last 1900 years. With these tools now available, no effort should be spared in correcting every mistranslation and in clarifying every misinterpretation of the inspired text.[6]

THE ONLY DISTINCTIVE THAT MATTERS

There is one distinctive that we Pentecostals should embrace with satisfaction. That is the fact that we are a people of the *anointing*, a people who recognize, honor, and are under the leadership and guidance of the Holy Spirit. That is, we expect the Holy Spirit to do something. That should be the only distinctive necessary to justify our existence. Anything else is incidental.

In every spectrum of the larger church, our emphasis on the anointing, empowerment, and leadership of the Spirit has thrust to the forefront of Christian thinking matters pertaining to the person and work of the Holy Spirit. That is significant! MacDonald, recognizing this truth, has stated:

> One of the chief contributions that Pentecostal theology has to make to the church at large stems from its championing of a dynamic experience of God. Belief in the availability of God's preternatural power and presence is foundational. It means a theology of a God-near-at-hand, who gives abundant evidence of His powerful presence in the church. This theology concerns itself with a deep and on-going experience in God.[7]

Colin Kruse has correctly noted: the dramatic growth and widespread influence of the charismatic (Neo-Pentecostal) movement this century has forced many to re-examine their understanding of the role of the Spirit in the early Christian community.[8]

---

6. Bivin and Blizzard, *Difficult Words,* 117; see also Pinnock, *Scripture Principle,* 206–7.

7. MacDonald, "Pentecostal Theology," 62.

8. Kruse, *Models for Ministry,* 4; see also Mills, *Glossolalia,* 121.

Indeed, is our position in the larger Church so tenuous, are our collective egos so fragile, that we need to claim uniqueness? What exactly is the motivation that lies behind this need to be distinctive, rather than taking our God-given and ordained place in the larger church he has established in the earth?

The term distinctive bears upon it the connotation of being *special.* Are we actually special in the sense that God cares more for us than for the rest of Christ's body on the earth? Are we special in the sense that God has granted to us a revelation of his person and purpose that he has not revealed to any other Christian group? Do we really want to claim that for ourselves? If that is the connotation attached to our use of the term, then we are to be pitied. Either we stand with all Christians, past, present, and future, within the stream of salvation history, or we need not lay claim to the name Christian. We must acknowledge that we stand on the shoulders of untold millions of God's saints who have made this sojourn before us, most of whom we would not label as being pentecostal, and that we are but an infinitesimal part of the overall history of the church of Jesus Christ. This is not said to denigrate Pentecostal history nor the value of our tenets of faith, rather, merely to remind us Pentecostals that the revelation of God in Christ did not begin with our twentieth-century movement and shall not end with it. In the overall picture of Christ's church we are but a drop in the bucket. The church of Jesus Christ was here when we arrived upon the scene, and it will be here if we are gone.

If we insist on claiming this uniqueness, we must be reminded that being *special* with God brings with it a tremendous burden of responsibility, denoting that we must become the leadership of the entire Christian church. We must be the example to the rest of the larger church in all of its life and ministry, not just in spirituality. We had better think that through before we take to ourselves that responsibility. Israel believed they were a people called by God to be special, but only in the sense of privilege; responsibility lay far from their minds. I wonder, do we Pentecostals share that mindset?

THE NATURE OF THE TASK

In any theological task such as the one before us it is imperative that we start from the right place. If we fail to do this we will necessarily arrive at some wrong conclusions and end with a deficient theology.

First, we shall examine the phenomenon of glossolalia as it occurred prior to the day of Pentecost among the adherents of the Hellenistic religions of the Greco/Roman world. We will also give consideration to the post-Pentecost events recorded in patristic literature and in the history of the followers of Edward Irving. The purpose of such a study is to fix in our thinking the fact that glossolalia is not simply a twentieth-century phenomenon and, therefore, we who stand in the stream of present history must realize that we do not have a lock on all that could or should be said relative to it. It is essential that we open our minds to what can be learned from these former manifestations of glossolalia.

We will also explore the theological stance of three traditions relative to Spirit-baptism and glossolalia: the Evangelical/Fundamentalist position, the classical Pentecostal position, and finally the Neo-Pentecostal position. This exploration will provide us with a comprehensive view of contemporary thought on the subject.

Then our task will focus on an examination of the present classical Pentecostal evidential constructs, their theological bases and hermeneutical difficulties, with particular emphasis on the *normative* argument.

Finally, we will endeavor to work through a comprehensive evidential construct for Spirit-baptism by examining the *biblical evidential paradigm* and the evidential construct embodied in the Pauline corpus. This will lead us to an understanding of the ultimate evidence of being Spirit-baptized people—an evidence that cannot be imitated by the demonic nor mimicked by the flesh; an evidence which the Spirit of God and he alone can produce in the believer's life.

PART ONE

Antecedents of Glossolalia

1

Glossolalia in the Hellenistic Religions

T HIS WRITER WAS BAPTIZED with the Holy Spirit at the age of thirteen
and spoke in tongues, and I still speak in tongues. It is my desire
to affirm here my personal belief in the validity and value of speaking
in tongues. This spiritual gift supplies the believer with a medium of
communication with God that no other charism of the Spirit provides.
With the Apostle Paul, I too desire that all speak in tongues (1 Cor 14:5).
Glossolalia, manifested by the Holy Spirit, is a gift of God that must not
be denigrated or suppressed.

However, having made that affirmation, I wish to state that it is imperative that we who believe in this phenomenon and have experienced
it in our day deal forthrightly with the facts of history. It may come as a
surprise for some to discover that the glossolalic phenomenon has a pre-
Pentecost history. The experience of the emerging church on the day of
Pentecost was *not* the introduction of speaking in tongues into the realm
of human experience.

During the research phase of this project I had occasion to review
many books written on the subject of glossolalia. Some were written by
Pentecostals, others by Charismatics, and some by non-Pentecostals. Very
few of these reviewed works mentioned the glossolalic phenomena associated with the Hellenistic religions of the ancient Greco/Roman period.[1]

PRE-PENTECOST GLOSSOLALIA

There is ample material available to deal with the basic historical facts
of the Hellenistic religions. The fact that some were secret orders does
abridge our knowledge to a great degree. However, thanks to ancient authors such as Plato, Homer, and many others (and to the modern scholars

1. Bach, *Inner Ecstasy*, 72–76; see also Mills, *Glossolalia*, 19–23, 77–88.

who have made these ancient writers accessible), we do have some valid information that archaeological discoveries have affirmed to be reliable. Since my concern here is with the historical references to glossolalia, I will not burden the reader with unnecessary historical data that does not bear upon the matter before us.

Joseph Fontenrose informs us that the Delphic Oracle, associated with the religion of Apollo, was well known for its emphasis on glossolalic phenomena[2] and was active for more than one thousand years. Parke and Wormell confirm Fontenrose when they observe, "The foundation of Delphi and its oracle took place before the times of recorded history."[3] Frederick Conybeare has informed us: the gift of tongues and of their interpretation was not peculiar to the Christian church but was a repetition in it of a phenomenon common in ancient religions. The very phrase *glossais lalein*, "to speak with tongues," was not invented by the New Testament writers but borrowed from ordinary speech.[4] Frederick Poulsen, in his discussion of the Delphic Oracle comments:

> Before the inspiration there were great preparations; the priestess fasted, bathed in Castalia, chewed laurel-leaves or inhaled the vapors of burnt laurel and myrrh. For her sooth-saying was "artless, unlearned," not like augury, or the investigation of entrails, an art and science practiced for generations. It was pure possession by the god, like that of Cassandra in the *Agamemnon* of Aeschylus or of the disciples in the Acts of the Apostles.[5]

While we Christians hold that there is a vast difference between the Delphic Oracle and the apostolic experience, it seems apparent that the oracles not only spoke in tongues but that their utterances were also interpreted, much like the practice recorded in the New Testament scriptures. The oracle was a woman who was referred to as the *Pythia*. According to Greek thought it was through her that the *god* spoke to the people. She was the direct connection to the god; the spirit of the god possessed her on these occasions. It was while she was in the state of *ecstasy* or *enthusiasm* that the god uttered his glossolalic communication. (Ecstasy or enthusiasm, as used in these religions, meant that state of religious

2. Fontenrose, *Delphic Oracle*, 6.

3. Parke and Wormell, *Delphic Oracle*, 2:3.

4. Conybeare, "Gift of Tongues".

5. Poulsen, *Delphi*, 23.

experience where the person was possessed by the god.) Following this message in tongues, "The Pythia's (priestess) utterance was interpreted by the prophets, i.e. the priests of Apollo."[6]

W. D. Davies apprises us that the *pneumatikos* in the Hellenistic religions is one who has had the vision of God that "gives an intimate personal insight into ultimate reality." This person possessed the highly prized *knosis* and was contrasted with the natural man, who did not possess *knosis*—the *psychikos*.[7]

The cult of Dionysus, also known for ecstatic phenomena, was another element of the Hellenistic religions. The mystery rites of this cult go back to the pre-Hellenic period. The cult, though an entity in itself, was loosely related to the religion of Apollo. According to Greek mythology, Zeus was the greatest of the Olympian gods. Apollo was the son of Zeus, and Dionysus was Apollo's younger brother. Of these gods, Dionysus was considered to be the mystic, ecstatic god. Ecstasy was an expected phenomena of this cult.[8] The priestess of Dionysus carried the title *Thyia*, which means, *the ecstatically raging*. This ecstasy included vocal expressions not understood by onlookers

Marcus Bach informs us that it was not just the priestess who spoke in tongues in this cult but that it appeared to be a common event during the festivals of the Eleusinian and Dionysian mysteries:

> When the exuberance of the worshipers reached rapturous heights, the incredible, sometimes musical utterances, began. They were like sounding brass and tinkling cymbal. The speakers became the center of attraction. Initiates listened enthralled and often they, too, became overpowered and burst into a babble of sounds. These Greek festivals flourished during the Golden Age, the prehistoric period ruled over by Cromus, god of the harvest. In these extravaganzas, held in spring and fall at planting and reaping time, devotees not only spoke in tongues but were also baptized in the rivers.[9]

Bach further observes that the glossolalic sounds were frequently made by the tongue alone. There was no voice, no speech, simply tongue talk—nonverbal sounds made with the tongue.

---

6. Ibid., 24 (parenthetical insertion mine).

7. Davies, *Paul*, 191.

8. Hoyle, *Delphi*, 74.

9. Bach, *Inner Ecstasy*, 72–73.

John McClintock and James Strong attest that the priestesses of these Hellenistic religions were as if possessed by a power they could not resist. "The wild unearthly sounds (*nec mortale sonans*), often hardly coherent, burst from their lips. It remained for the interpreter to collect the scattered utterances and give them meaning."[10]

THE MYSTERIES AT CORINTH

There is strong support for the idea that the church at Corinth was composed of believers who had come to Christ predominantly from the Hellenistic religions. H. Wayne House cites three possible sources for this: the Cybele-Attis cult, the Dionysian cult, and the religion of Apollo. Of these possibilities the Dionysian cult and the religion of Apollo appear to be the probable sources.

> With the ecstacism of Dionysianism and the emphasis on tongues-speaking and oracles in the religion of Apollo, it is not surprising that some of the Corinthians carried these pagan ideas into the church at Corinth, especially the practice of glossolalia for which both of these religions are known (though the Dionysian cult did not include interpretation of the glossolalia as did that of Apollo).[11]

House points to this as a possible explanation for Paul's dilemma with the excessive tongues-speech at Corinth. He believes that the inordinate use of tongues there was a direct carryover from the former religious practices in the mysteries, with their inordinate emphasis on glossolalia, which was viewed as being a sign that one was possessed by the god.[12]

We have engaged in this brief junket into the history of pre-Pentecost glossolalia, as used in these religions, to demonstrate from a historical perspective that there are pre-Pentecost manifestations of the glossolalic phenomena in human experience, and that speaking in tongues is not a phenomenon associated only with Christian experience.

---

10. McClintock and Strong, "Gift of Tongues," 485.
11. House, "Tongues," 138.
12. Ibid., 134.

THE SOURCE OF PRE-PENTECOST GLOSSOLALIA

We must now determine the source of these glossolalic manifestations. Are these manifestations the same as those experienced by the early church and by Pentecostals/Charismatics in our day?

First and foremost, it should be emphasized that the glossolalic manifestations in these religions are similar but certainly not the same as true Holy Spirit produced expressions in Christian life and worship. It is possible that much of the frenzy over tongues-speech in the Corinthian church was merely fleshly demonstration. However, the genuine expression of the Spirit should not be confused with such manifestations. And that appears to be the very point Paul desired to make with the Corinthian church.

Parke and Wormell address the question of the source of glossolalia in these religions and propose two theories: either it was a product of subliminal human consciousness or, as the ancient Christian apologists maintained, it was demonic.[13]

Pentecostals would probably identify the distinction as either of the *flesh* or the demonic. In other words, the flesh can mimic Holy Spirit produced glossolalia, and the demonic can imitate this phenomenon.

To be sure, we would not label such an expression, that is, one not produced by the Holy Spirit, as necessarily demonic. It may instead be a product of the *flesh,* and we should label it accordingly. In other words, we do affirm in our theology that the *flesh* can mimic glossolalic manifestation and that this can occur within the framework of a Pentecostal believer's life and our corporate worship. This fact is embedded in our tradition. It was recognized by the pioneers of twentieth-century Pentecost, Charles and Sarah Parham. In 1903, approximately two years following the initial outpouring of the Spirit at their Bible school in Topeka, Kansas, the Parhams were conducting meetings at Nevada, Missouri, where they, for what appears to be the first time, "saw some fleshly manifestations, and giving out of messages we had not witnessed before."

Following this event Mrs. Parham relates this experience: "One day, when in prayer, a power seized my lower jaw, which began to tremble, then shake with increased violence. Mr. Parham came to the door. He did not condemn or criticize but I knew he was praying silently. The power, over which I had not control, left me and I realized it was not of God."[14]

---

13. Parke and Wormell, *Delphic Oracle,* 36–37.

14. Parham, *Charles F. Parham,* 87.

Approximately three years later, the Parhams confronted this problem on a large scale in Los Angeles at the famed Azusa Street Mission. W. J. Seymour had been pleading with Parham for some time to come out to California from Kansas to help stem the tide of fanaticism that had grasped control there. Parham informs us:

> I hurried to Los Angeles, and to my utter surprise and astonishment I found conditions even worse than I had anticipated. Brother Seymour came to me helpless, he said he could not stem the tide that had arisen. I sat on the platform in Azusa Street Mission, and saw the manifestations of the flesh, spiritualistic controls, saw people practicing hypnotism at the altar over candidates seeking the baptism; though many were receiving the real baptism of the Holy Ghost.[15]

Parham continues:

> Let me speak plainly with regard to the work as I have found it here. I found hypnotic influences, familiar-spirit influences, spiritualistic influences, mesmeric influences, and all kinds of spells, spasms, falling in trances, etc. All of these things are foreign to and unknown in this movement outside of Los Angeles, except in the places visited by the workers sent out from this city.[16]

Parham further observes:

There are many in Los Angeles who sing, pray and talk wonderfully in other tongues, as the Spirit gives utterance, and there is jabbering here that is not tongues at all. I know that people sometimes fall under the power of God, and that there are times that God thus deals with his creatures that resist Him; but these cases are exceptional, and are not general. The falling under the power in Los Angeles has, to a large degree, been produced through hypnotic, mesmeric, magnetic current.[17]

The point to be made here is this: the fact that someone manifests the glossolalic phenomenon does not ensure that they are expressing a manifestation of the Holy Spirit.

They may be operating out of their soulishness, that is, their *flesh*. And depending on the person, we might want to say it was demonic. This truth is something that we Pentecostals are, indeed, aware of and that we must

15. Ibid., 163

16. Ibid., 168.

17. Ibid, 169.

come to terms with, relative to our beliefs about Spirit-baptism. R. Hollis Gause maintains that true Spirit produced glossolalia is not a learned or practiced response, nor is it humanly initiated. Spirit produced tongues-speech make such human actions unnecessary. They substitute the human will for the divine will. They impose human gibberish and nonsense syllables for the oracle of God. Our efforts to imitate the work of God interfere with the work of the Holy Spirit and reject his sovereignty.[18] In this manner, Gause acknowledges the fact of fleshly manifestations of glossolalia and insists that such human activity impedes the true work of the Holy Spirit.[19]

A SUMMARY

The facts of history demonstrate to us that this phenomenon was used for hundreds of years by the Hellenistic religions and that in those instances it was produced either by Satanic influences or through the psychic impulses of the *flesh*. The facts of history inform us that the flesh and the demonic were manifesting counterfeits of real Spirit produced glossolalia in the early years of the pentecostal outpouring in America. Gause cautions us to avoid fleshly demonstrations purporting to be of the Spirit. The data presented above gives us good cause to rethink what we believe about the evidence for Spirit-baptism. The belief that speaking in tongues is the *primary evidence* that one has been filled with the Holy Spirit is at best tenuous. We must seek an evidential construct or constructs that can be neither mimicked by the flesh nor imitated by the demonic. But, you might say, our tenets of faith say that glossolalia is only the *initial evidence,* or the initial *physical* evidence, of Spirit-baptism, depending on the formulation of a particular statement of faith. In most cases where this is true, however, the problem is this: all too often those terms translate into absolute concepts in the minds of those who use them. Hence, *initial physical evidence* equals the *primary evidence* of being Spirit baptized. And though one may manifest other gifts of the Spirit without speaking in an unknown tongue, it usually is intimated, if not outright insisted upon, that such a person does not have the Holy Spirit resident within. But we shall deal with this matter further in chapter 9.

---

18. Gause, *Living in the Spirit*, 85.

19. See also Ewald, "Aspects of Tongues," 12–13, 19.

2

Glossolalia in the Patristic Literature

TURNING NOW TO PATRISTIC literature, our purpose here is to discover the thought of various church fathers relative to glossolalia. Did it occur in their time? If so, what importance did they place upon the phenomenon? Is there any hint in this literature that speaking in tongues should be considered a primary evidence of being filled with the Holy Spirit? Is there an indication of any particular evidence being set forth as *the* evidence of being Spirit filled? The answers we glean from this literature relative to the above posed questions should give us some direction as we struggle with the question of an adequate evidential construct for Spirit-baptism.

However, it would be well if at this juncture we heed the observation of Pentecostal scholar Harold Hunter: "The writings of the apostolic fathers are primarily pastoral—not theological—in orientation."[1] Therefore, we cannot seek to redact into their writings certain theological constructs we may desire to reinforce, either in favor of tongues or in opposition to tongues.

Hunter further notes, relative to this literature: "While it would be presumptuous to assume all patristic doctrines to be biblical, the prestige of the Fathers demands that attention be paid to their assessment of any doctrine that claims to be biblical."[2]

A REDISCOVERED THEOLOGY OF THE SPIRIT?

Reflection on the stance of Pentecostals relative to a theology of the Spirit, reveals that we have conveyed to the larger Christian community the idea that we have *rediscovered* the early church's teaching on the person and

1. Hunter, "Tongues-Speech," 125.
2. Hunter, *Spirit-Baptism*, 117.

work of the Holy Spirit. Carl Brumback, in discussing the *recovery* of New Testament truth, conveys the idea that modern Pentecostalism has recaptured doctrine lost during the dark hours of the church's history. Speaking of the Reformers he states, "It seems that they, and their successors as well, had blind spots in their spiritual vision. Some portions of truth were hidden from them, awaiting another hour for their full revelation."[3] He continues in that vein, making explicit claim that the modern Pentecostal movement has made such a recovery: "Precept was upon precept, line upon line, here a little and there a little, as God patiently led His Church back to the New Testament standard of *doctrine* and religious experience."[4]

I sometimes think we actually believe this to be true; therefore, we have the last word on any matter pertaining to the Holy Spirit. It is almost as if the Spirit were some sort of private domain of Pentecostals. Fortunately, that is a misconception.

A perusal of Church history will set the record straight in this regard. Stanley Burgess, a Pentecostal historian, informs us that "among those doctrines which remained largely undeveloped in the pre-Nicene period was that of the Holy Spirit."[5] William Rusch points out that there was not a full blown theology of the Spirit present in the early church. There was not even a consensus regarding the person and work of the Spirit. Tertullian (d.c. 220) is the first Father prior to the fourth century to present a theology of the Spirit in a clear and precise manner.[6]

The early history of the church reveals a considerable divergence of views about the Holy Spirit. While it is accurate to acknowledge that by the time of scholasticism such dissimilitude had sharply decreased, homogeneity did not result. In fact, down to our own day churches of the East and West retain different points of view about the third person of the Trinity.[7]

It was primarily the influence of heresy that forced the church of the patristic era to begin its theological labors on matters of the Spirit, and this did not occur until the year 300. Rusch has called this a matter of *benign neglect* on the part of the church. He cites an observation by

---

3. Brumback, *What Meaneth This?* 278.

4. Ibid.

5. Burgess, *Spirit and the Church,* 12.

6. Rusch, *Holy Spirit,* 72.

7. Ibid., 66.

Jaroslav Pelikan, who said, "At Nicea the doctrine of the Holy Spirit had been disposed of in lapidary brevity: 'And we believe in the Holy Spirit.'"[8]

Rusch further observes: "This succinctness discloses that even in the early phases of the Arian controversy attention was so fixed on the Son that little reference was made to the Spirit, apart from affirming the traditional work of the Spirit. This is true for the creeds as late as the year 360."[9]

It is a mistaken notion, then, to assume that twentieth-century Pentecostals have *rediscovered* the New Testament church's teaching on the Holy Spirit, since there was not a body of church doctrine that could be so labeled and conveyed to future generations. What we Pentecostals possess today, as a body of doctrine concerning the person and work of the Spirit, is actually certain theological concepts formulated by twentieth-century believers in an effort to explain, in biblical terms, what had happened to them in their twentieth-century experience of the Holy Spirit. This should cause us to approach this matter in a spirit of openness and humility, with teachable spirits and a great sense of charity.

Harold Hunter has written one of the most extensive works on tongues-speech as it is dealt with in patristic writings. His scholarly and copiously documented piece, *Tongues-Speech: A Patristic Analysis*, appeared in the *Journal of the Evangelical Theological Society* in June 1980.

Hunter argues that Irenaeus mentions the glossolalic phenomenon when he writes, "The apostle says, 'We speak wisdom among those that are perfect,' calling those perfect who have received the Spirit of God and who speak in all tongues through the Spirit, just as he himself spoke, and just as we hear many brethren in the Church, who have the prophetic charismata and who by the Spirit, speak all kinds of tongues . . . whom the apostle terms spiritual."[10]

Tertullian appears to encourage the exercise of glossolalia in his comment, "When he mentions the fact that 'it is written in the law, how that the Creator would speak with other tongues and other lips, whilst confirming indeed the gift of tongues by such a mention.'"[11]

Several brief, well written pieces by Andrew T. Floris have appeared in various issues of *Paraclete*. He points out that Macarius of Egypt (300–390),

8. Ibid., 74.

9. Ibid.

10. Irenaeus quoted in Hunter, "Tongues-Speech," 129.

11. Tertullian, *Against Marcion*, 5.8.

"in his *Fifty Spiritual Homilies* makes many references to the gifts of the Spirit as they are enumerated by the apostle Paul in 1 Corinthians 12–14. He states that the gifts were manifested, in his time, in the lives of many."[12]

Hunter observes, "The work entitled *Fifty Homilies of Macarius of Egypt* was most probably not authored by Macarius but by someone unknown to us. Speaking of his own day the writer (*Homily* 36:1) specifies tongues as one of the gifts of the Spirit and tells (*Homily* 29:1) about some who possessed gifts of the Spirit but *failed because they fell short of love.*"[13]

Novation referred to the contemporary practice of spiritual gifts, where tongues is specifically mentioned: "This is he who places prophets in the church, instructs teachers, directs tongues, gives powers and healing . . . and arranges whatever other gifts there are of the charismata."[14]

Hunter tells us that the Cappadocian fathers, all of whom had been monks, uniformly spoke of the contemporary exercise of *charismata* and perhaps also tongues-speech. Gregory Nazianzen talked (*Oration* 32; PCC 36:185; *Oration on Pentecost* 41:12; *On the Holy Spirit* 5:12:30) about the charismata and perhaps tongues-speech as still present in his day. Likewise, Gregory of Nyssa spoke frequently of this charismata.[15]

In his discussion of Basil and the gifts of the Spirit, Floris informs us that, according to Basil, the Holy Spirit arranges, directs, and adorns the church with various gifts. The Paraclete leads into all truth and establishes all who believe in sure knowledge and accurate confession as well as in spiritual and true worship of the triune God. Basil says, "God works the differences of operations, and the Lord the diversities of administrations, but all the while the Holy Spirit is present too of His own will, dispensing distribution of the gifts according to each recipient's worth." He then quotes 1 Corinthians 12:4–6, 11.

In his homily *On Faith,* which in reality is a Confession of Faith, Basil declares, "We believe therefore and confess one only true and good God . . . and one only Spirit, the Paraclete . . . Who divideth and worketh the gifts that come from God." And his sixth homily on "The Hexaemeron" concludes with the prayer that the manifestation of the Holy Spirit be granted to his congregation according to the proportion of their faith.

---

12. Floris, "Spiritual Gifts," 18.

13. Hunter, "Tongues-Speech," 132 (emphasis mine).

14. Quoted in Hunter, "Tongues-Speech," 131.

15. Hunter, "Tongues-Speech," 133.

In his *Shorter Rules*, No. 278, answering the question, "How does a man's spirit pray while his understanding remains without fruit?" Basil states, "This was said concerning those that utter their prayer in a tongue unknown to the hearers." Floris notes here that the verb *utter* is in the present tense. There can be no doubt that at least some believers were exercising this gift. Elsewhere, Basil exhorts and directs the faithful to follow the evangelical pattern of worship as portrayed in the Pauline epistles: "Rather we should imitate the conventions which are recorded in the Gospels of our Lord Jesus Christ, and fulfill what the apostle commands as conducive to the following of such a model." Thus he writes, "When ye come together, each of you hath a psalm, hath a teaching, hath a revelation, hath a tongue, hath an interpretation; but let all things be done unto edifying."[16]

It is of interest to note that W. K. Lowther Clarke, in his work on Basil, makes this observation regarding Basil's idea of the evidence of the presence of the Spirit in the life of the believer:

> Basil had drunk too deeply of the well of the gospel truth to make mistakes about the charismata. In F.3 where he is discussing the New Testament evidence, not from an academic standpoint, but as describing something which applied to his own time, he says that *the Lord asked for love as the sign and test of discipleship*, not signs and wonders, though He gives these in the Holy Ghost.[17]

According to Hunter, though Augustine did not believe in contemporary practice of glossolalia, he does make this significant statement relative to the phenomenon,

> In the earlier times, the Holy Ghost fell upon them that believed and they spake with tongues, which they had not learned, "as the Spirit gave them utterance." These signs were adapted to the times, for there behooved to be that betokening of the Holy Spirit in all tongues, to show that the Gospel of God was to run through all tongues over the whole earth. If then the witness of the presence of the Holy Ghost be not given through these miracles, what is it given? . . . *If he loves his brother, the Spirit of God dwelleth in him.*[18]

---

16. Floris, "The Charismata," 11–12.

17. Clarke, *Ascetic Works*, 96 (emphasis mine).

18. Hunter, "Tongues-Speech," 134 (emphasis mine).

With this brief review of what some of the patristic writings reveal concerning the thought of these believers regarding glossolalia, we can respond to the questions posed at the outset of this chapter.

A SUMMARY

First, did the phenomena occur in their time? It is apparent from these writings that tongues-speech was contemporary for the majority of the authors reviewed. It was part and parcel of the charismata experienced by believers during this period, though it might not have been a common practice for all Christians everywhere.

Second, what importance did they assign tongues-speech? It would appear that they did not consider the phenomenon to be a primary aspect of the charismata. Nothing is said that could lend itself to such a conclusion. It apparently was valued as a part of the charismata but not singled out as an indicator of significance. It certainly was not looked upon as something belonging to the early church as an aid to its establishment and then done away with (although we do acknowledge that there was a statement made to that effect by Augustine).

Third, is there any hint in this literature that speaking in tongues should be considered a primary evidence that one is Spirit-filled? As has been shown above, there is no such notion in the writings reviewed, and any such notion derived from these Fathers would certainly be mere interpolation on the part of the observer.

Fourth, is there an indication of *any* particular evidence set forth by these authors as to the presence of the fullness of the Spirit in a believer's life? Here we can answer in the affirmative. We found in Macarius of Egypt, Basil, and Augustine the concept that *love* was an evidence that the Holy Spirit was present in a person's life.

3

Glossolalia in Nineteenth-Century England

THE PARTICULAR HISTORICAL ANTECEDENT under consideration here will be Edward Irving and his followers, otherwise known as the Catholic Apostolic Church. As we turn our attention to this antecedent of contemporary glossolalia we shall pursue the same questions asked of the patristic literature. Was glossolalia a phenomenon current in this time period? Should that be the case, what importance did the church attach to the phenomenon? Is there any indication here that speaking in tongues should be considered the *primary* evidence that one has been Spirit-filled? Is there an indication that any particular evidence is considered to be *the evidence* of being Spirit-filled? As with our queries of the patristic literature, the answers gleaned here may also give us direction in our pursuit of an adequate evidential construct for Spirit-baptism.

THE HISTORICAL MILIEU

Edward Irving was educated at Edinburgh University. His course of study was the usual rigorous Scottish educational fare. He describes what the program was like:

> In respect of the ministers, this was required of them—that they should have studied for four years in a University all the branches of a classical and philosophical education, and either taken the rank in literature of a Master of Arts, or come out from the University with a certificate of their proficiency in the classics, in mathematics, in logic, and in natural and moral philosophy.
>
> They are then, and not until then, permitted to enter upon the study of theology, of which the professors are ordained ministers of the Church, chosen to their office. Under separate professors they study theology, Hebrew, and ecclesiastical history for four

years, attending from four to six months a year. Thus eight years
are consumed in study.[1]

Irving became the pastor of a little Church of Scotland congregation,
Caledonian Chapel, Cross Street, Hatton Garden, London, on October 16,
1822. (Prior to this he was the assistant to Dr. Thomas Chalmers in St.
John's parish, Glasgow.)

In a very short time the dynamic preaching of Irving had drawn the
attention of people from every strata of society. His sermons were long
and dealt with the sins of the people, yet this did not daunt those eager
to hear this young Scottish orator. In two years the little chapel in Hatton
Garden no longer held the crowds who came to hear Irving preach,
and a new building was erected in Regent Square, the National Scotch
Church, which served as a national cathedral representing the Church
of Scotland in the metropolis.[2] The new Regent Square building was, as
Andrew L. Drummond notes, "by far the finest place of worship outside
the Establishment in London."[3]

It is clear that Edward Irving was not some offbeat *fringy* as some
would make him appear. Rather, he was a respected, honored, and well
educated man of the cloth. Powerful preaching was Irving's forte; however, he was known for his pastoral expertise as well. Lutheran scholar
Larry Christenson notes that "Irving's gifts as a pastor—a shepherd of
souls—were more impressive still and stood somewhat in contrast to his
flamboyant oratorical style."[4]

Irving first became the focus of controversy in 1828 following the
publication of a book of sermons on the Incarnation of Christ. His thesis
was on the humanity of Christ, and his treatment of that topic created
a great stir and eventually was the cause of his being censured and de-
frocked by the London Presbytery for heresy. However, the session of his
church overruled the Presbytery's judgment and kept him on as pastor.

Irving seemed to draw controversy like a magnet. He had taken the
standard Reformed position that the charismata had ceased with the passing of the last apostle. But that was soon to change. In March or April of
1830, after being ill and bed-ridden for about 18 months, Mary Campbell

1. Oliphant, Edward Irving, 33.

2. Drummond, *Irving and His Circle*, 44.

3. Ibid., 103.

4. Christenson, *Charismatic Movement*, 33.

and Margaret MacDonald, whom he had known back home in Scotland, were miraculously healed. After this occurred they had a series of visions. This got Irving's attention. Margaret claimed to have seen visions of the coming of the Lord. She wrote down these visions and sent a copy to Irving. A month later (June of 1830), Irving claimed in a private letter that the visions had made a huge impact on him relative to the charismata. "The substance of Mary Campbell's and Margaret MacDonald's visions or revelations, given in their papers, carry to me a spiritual conviction and a spiritual reproof which I cannot express."

Along with the contentions of his associate, Alexander J. Scott, that the charismata were being restored to the church, these events convinced Irving of the validity of the contemporary workings of the Holy Spirit. God was restoring charismatic gifts in their own age.[5]

Approximately one year following these events, Mrs. Cardale, wife of prominent London attorney, J. B. Cardale, head of Cardale, Iliffe & Russell, manifested the gifts of tongues and interpretation.[6] From there the charismata continued to develop in the Regent Square congregation. In the beginning Irving did not permit the use of tongues and interpretation in the public services. It was, rather, confined to the midweek service where, Irving states in a letter to a friend, "every Wednesday night I am preaching to thousands 'the Baptism with the Holy Spirit,' and the Lord is mightily with us."[7]

Because Irving, who had been preaching on the work of the Holy Spirit, genuinely believed these expressions to be the work of the Spirit, he would not quell these charismatic outbursts, which now pervaded even the public worship services. His reticence to stop the pentecostal manifestations in public caused the trustees of the church to appeal to the London Presbytery for assistance in stopping what they viewed to be the exercise of public ministry by unauthorized persons. On May 4, 1832, Irving was again found guilty and removed from the ministry of the Church of Scotland. This action by the London Presbytery prompted the exodus of the majority of the membership of the National Church

---

5. Hunter, *Spirit-Baptism*, 175.

6. Drummond, *Irving and His Circle*, 153.

7. Hunter, *Spirit-Baptism*, 176.

(1500–2000 members) in Regent Square who, with Irving, formed the Catholic Apostolic Church.[8]

The ideas of this man and these people will be the focus of our attention as we continue our pursuit for understanding in the matter of glossolalia and its relationship to Spirit-baptism.

Historical occurrences of the glossolalic phenomenon, subsequent to those in the early church, most often were occasioned by extreme religious enthusiasm and evangelical fervor. However, this cannot be stated in the case of Irving and the Catholic Apostolic Church. Gordon Strachan, a Pentecostal scholar, notes:

> Nothing could be further from the truth, for unlike any previous manifestations of the Spirit, they were occasioned not by the overflow of powerful religious feeling but by faithful response to the systematic study and preaching of the Word of God. Theological understanding was central to all that happened and preceded all forms of experience of spiritual gifts. It is the centrality of a coherent theological system which makes the Pentecost of 1830–32 unique and quite distinct from all previous revivals.[9]

Since this nineteenth-century Pentecostal movement rose out of a developed theological system, it is of primary importance for this study. One might expect to find within the body of doctrine developed through this theology specific statements relative to glossolalia and Spirit-baptism, and indeed, we do find such statements. They must bear a great deal of significance for twentieth-century Pentecostals if we are to stay in touch with historic Christian developments and not lose our way in the labyrinth of modern Pentecostal assumptions and presuppositions.

EDWARD IRVING'S POSITION ON GLOSSOLALIA

Regarding Irving's personal position concerning tongues-speech, Harold Hunter makes this observation: Modern writers from the Charismatic movement make the claim that Irving believed tongues to be the special evidence of Spirit-baptism. Irving is quoted as saying of the doctrine of the baptism with the Holy Spirit that its "standing sign, if we err not, is the speaking with tongues."[10]

8. Strachan, *Theology of Edward Irving*, 13–14.

9. Strachan, *Theology of Edward Irving*, 14–15.

10. Hunter, *Spirit-Baptism*, 178.

Noting that "Irving himself never spoke in tongues,"[11] Hunter makes this succinct point:

> One could say that if this be true, then Irving would have to be-
> lieve that he was never Spirit-baptized. The following authorities
> say that Irving did not speak in tongues: Williams and Waldvogel,
> "Tongues," 86; Cutten, *Tongues*, 100; Christenson, "Forerunner," 19;
> Damboriena, *Tongues*, 189, n48; Dave MacPherson, *The Incredible
> Cover-up* (Plainfield: Logos, 1975) 29.[12]

Christenson concurs with this view, citing Drummond's quotation of Irving:

> Again, no one doubteth that Christian baptism doth convey to the
> believer the gift of repentance towards God, and the remission of
> sins by the regeneration of the Holy Spirit: and why should they
> doubt that it doth convey also the baptism with the Holy Spirit for
> speaking with tongues and prophesying?[13]

Irving made many other statements that do seem to indicate that he considered tongues-speech primary in Spirit-baptism. Hunter comments that "it is quite true that tongues were an important part of Spirit-bap-tism according to Irving."[14] The following are some further comments by Irving relative to tongues-speech and Spirit-baptism:

> We find it (tongues) always to have been the gift first bestowed
> upon the baptized (Acts 2, 10:46, 19:1) and in the instances now
> appearing in the Church, this is the only gift which hath been giv-
> en.... that the utterance of tongues which no one understandeth ..
> . is the forthcoming of the soul filled with the Holy Ghost ... there
> is not any believer in the Lord Jesus Christ who ought not to desire
> and pray for, and who may not expect, the gift of tongues.[15]

"To announce the undoubted presence of God within us, there is the gift of tongues."[16]

---

11. Ibid., 179.

12. Ibid., 205.

13. Quoted in Drummond, *Irving and His Circle*, 164; cited by Christensen, *Charismatic Movement*, 56.

14. Hunter, *Spirit-Baptism*, 178.

15. Quoted in Hunter, *Spirit-Baptism*, 178.

16. Quoted in Strachan, *Theology of Edward Irving*, 98 (emphasis mine).

Though these quotes do appear to endorse the idea that tongues is *the* sign that one is Spirit-baptized, balance must be brought to Irving's views by citing the following explicit statement relative to Spirit-baptism and tongues-speech, in which he posits a disclaimer regarding the idea that all *must* speak in tongues to be Spirit-filled:

> That, *though it be not received, we should not be disheartened, as if we were rejected of the Holy Ghost, and had not the Holy Ghost dwelling in us*: because it is but the sign of a universal truth, concerning the communication between God and man, through Christ and the Holy Ghost, without any intervention; and that this is the only way through which the weary and heavy-laden sinner can come to rest; wherefore also the Holy Ghost is called the Comforter. If any person, therefore, having laid hold of this truth, is living in the faith and enjoyment of it, he is to be assured of his salvation, and to be at peace: yet he is to desire to speak with tongues, in order to convince an unbelieving and ignorant world, who will ever be trusting to book reading, or man-teaching, or self-sufficiency, or some other form of error, instead of trusting the indwelling operation of the Spirit of Christ.[17]

It is obvious from the above statement that Irving did not expect that every one would speak in tongues. Everyone certainly should *desire to speak with tongues*, since tongues are a sign to the unbeliever and the ignorant world that God has extended his incarnation, through Jesus Christ, to the believing church and does, indeed, indwell that church by his Holy Spirit. For Irving, Spirit-baptism is a universal truth: *"Of this baptism, we have already declared, that every mortal man is an heir, and every believer as possessor, whether he may have stirred up the gift or not."*[18]

Tongues is but a sign of this universal truth and does not serve as a guarantee of it. When Irving speaks of tongues as being the *standing sign,* he is not inferring the same connotation by that statement that we Pentecostals do when we speak of tongues as *the initial physical evidence* that one has been Spirit-baptized.

---

17. Edward Irving. "On the Gifts of the Holy Ghost, Commonly Called Supernatural." In *Morning Watch* Vols. 2 and 3, 560; cited by Strachan, *Edward Irving,* 104–5 (emphasis mine).

18. Irving, *Christ's Holiness,* 109–10; quoted in Strachan, *Theology of Edward Irving,* 97.

Coming from the Reformed theological tradition, Irving under-stands that one receives the fullness of the Spirit at one's baptism (water), as we see from the following statement,

> For baptism, Christ's ordinance, containeth two things, the work-ing away of our sin, and the baptism with the Holy Ghost; the former holding of redemption and satisfaction, the latter holding of the new acquisition which our nature made on the morning of Christ's baptism. I present, therefore, unto every man in Christ, not only deliverance from the old offense of Adam, with all its train of consequences, but also the new inheritance of the Holy Ghost, as a Spirit of power, the earnest of an inheritance whereof Adam's was only a type.[19]

Again, to properly understand Irving's statements on Spirit-baptism one must bear in mind that what he says has to be viewed in the light of his Reformed theological positions and not interpreted through twenti-eth-century Pentecostal or Charismatic glasses.

For Irving, the Spirit is received at the moment of one's water bap-tism. One receives the gift of justification, the removal of our sin, but at the same time one receives the baptism with the Holy Spirit. Here we see the confluence of two theological ideas that were responsible for Irving's censure by the Church of Scotland: the idea of Christ entering into and partaking of our humanity through the incarnation in order to redeem mankind and the next logical step beyond that incarnation—just as Jesus Christ partook of our nature and became truly man, we through him and by the Holy Spirit become partakers of the divine nature (Irving calls this the inhabitation of the Father) and manifests through our lives the same gifts of the Spirit expressed through Jesus' life, and greater than these.[20] Irving understood the *greater than these* to refer to speaking in tongues.[21]

It is apparent that Irving would not affirm modern day Pentecostal doctrine regarding Spirit-baptism on a wholesale basis. He would agree with parts of it but certainly not the idea that the new birth and Spirit-baptism are two distinct events—that one receives the Spirit (or the Spirit's fullness) after receiving the new birth.

---

19. Ibid.

20. See John 14:13.

21. Strachan, *Theology of Edward Irving*, 81.

Irving came to view the work of the Spirit in three operations (somewhat like the three stages understood by some Pentecostals of our day):

> As the operation of the Holy Ghost brought Christ into manhood, which is generation; so the continuance of that kind of operation brings the elect and believing ones of the Father forth from the bosom of his counsels unto Christ; and this is regeneration, conducted properly under the hand of the Father. Being brought unto Christ, another operation of the Holy Ghost doth wash and cleanse, and feed and nourish us up in him, upon his flesh and blood; and this is under the hand of the Son. . . . Then cometh the third and last operation of the Holy Ghost, which is baptism with the Holy Ghost, bringing into the believer, thus united with Christ, the fullness of that inhabitation of the Father which Christ now enjoys for ever. And this is the coming of the Father and the Son to dwell in us.[22]

Though he made these affirmations concerning the work of the Spirit, he still viewed this as being part and parcel of the *grace* one receives through water baptism. One receives the Spirit at the new birth, and the Spirit performs these operations in that person's life, as an ongoing process.

Irving would not concur with the notion that insists that one must speak in tongues in order to be Spirit-filled. In point of fact, those who succeeded Irving in the leadership of the movement did not hold to the idea that tongues stood as *the* evidence of Spirit-baptism.

THE CATHOLIC APOSTOLIC CHURCH'S POSITION ON GLOSSOLALIA

Christenson argues that the Catholic Apostolic Church *soft peddled* the charismatic manifestations, stating that the apostles of the church (the leaders who succeeded Irving) sought to disabuse them of the idea that because, earlier in the movement, the laying on of hands was in most cases followed by tongues and prophesying, therefore some outward manifestation or inward consciousness of spiritual grace or power was to be expected or looked for as proof of the reality of the gift concerned. After Irving's passing, speaking in tongues was not permitted in the public service, as it was believed to be disruptive. Apparently it was confined

22. Ibid., 125.

to smaller group meetings and private devotions, as had been the practice when the charismata were first manifested. In these later times, hardly an instance occurred of any individual commencing to speak with tongues or prophesy at the time of receiving the laying on of hands. Should such a case occur, it was necessary to stop it, as an interruption of the service.

The Catholic Apostolic Church, as we have seen, saw baptism as conveying spiritual *life* and the baptism with the Holy Spirit ("sealing") as conveying the *ability to minister* in the body of Christ, with no immediate charismatic manifestation, but a definite expectation of "fruit."[23]

It should be apparent to the reader that the leadership following Irving did not view tongues to be the primary evidence that one had been Spirit-filled. On the contrary, they played down the importance of any outward manifestation in relationship to Spirit-baptism and relied rather on the expression of fruit (the ethical dimension of the Spirit's work) as evidence that one had been Spirit-baptized. (The idea of fruit bearing necessarily demands love [agape] as its basis [1 Cor 13; Gal 5:22]. Love is primary and all other spiritual fruit grows out from it.)

A SUMMARY

From this brief excursion through the historical setting of the Catholic Apostolic Church and its founder, Edward Irving, we discover that Irving initially appears to endorse the idea that speaking in tongues was part and parcel of the baptism with the Holy Spirit and considered it to be *first* evidence, or primary indication that one had been Spirit-filled. However, closer examination of his theology reveals that this was not the case. Though he considered speaking with tongues to be valid and indeed important, he affirmed that the ethical evidence (fruit bearing) proved to be a more valid evidence of the Spirit-filled life than did the charismatic evidence in any form. This is seen, also, in the attitude of the apostles of the church who followed him in leadership of the movement.

We must conclude, then, that though glossolalia was considered to be of value and valid for all time, it was not held to be primary evidence that one had been Spirit-filled. The charismatic dimension was preempted by the ethical dimension. Proof that one had been baptized with the Holy Spirit (which occurred at the moment of water baptism) was that one evidenced in one's life the proofs of Galatians 5:22: love, joy, peace, patience,

23. Christenson, *Charismatic Movement*, 58–59, 62.

kindness, goodness, faithfulness, gentleness, and self control. All of these evidences rise out of the ethical dimension of our salvation, the holiness of Christ and his vicarious death on the cross, through which we too enter into that ethical dimension of true humanity provided by grace.

Though a full treatment of Irving's Pentecostal theology would not be appropriate in this work, it is apparent that this man's trained theological mind produced a system of thought relative to the things of the Spirit that we present day Pentecostals must give concerted attention to. A comprehensive treatment of Irving's theology has been set forth by Gordon Strachan in the book, *The Pentecostal Theology of Edward Irving.*

PART TWO

The Arguments of Three Traditions

4

The Traditionalist Position

THE TRADITIONAL POSITION IS represented by the Evangelical and Fundamentalist segments of the church. It has been set forth in writing, primarily by persons associated with Baptist persuasions and those who embrace Reformed theology, both reflecting Calvinist thought. Nearly all of the authors follow the same argument, and little can be discovered that is new or enlightening by moving from author to author.

A FEW PRESUPPOSITIONS

Each of the writers researched brings several presuppositions to the subject, some differing, some alike. First, the quality of Christian life and experience today is identical to that of the early church. Second, the church of the twentieth century has achieved, in some respects, a level of spiritual maturity far beyond that of the early church. Third, the Evangelical or Fundamentalist interpretation of Scripture is the only accurate and correct interpretation. Fourth, the charismatic gifts of the Holy Spirit were given to the newly birthed church to empower it but were later rescinded as the church matured. They are no longer needed.

There are other presuppositions, of course, but these are the most apparent and should be kept in mind in reviewing the position of these writers. For the sake of brevity this position shall be referred to as the traditionalist viewpoint throughout this chapter.

The traditionalists lay claim to biblical and hermeneutical accuracy in their treatment of glossolalia. They appeal to this often, insisting that beliefs must be based on the Word of God, but an approach to Scripture that relies heavily on reason, as theirs does, at the expense of the Spirit could be termed biblicist.

Jimmy A. Millikin, a Southern Baptist scholar, cites Carl Brumback, a Pentecostal, who takes the position that the doctrine of the Holy Spirit stands or falls on its basis in Scripture or the lack of it. Millikin agrees with this notion but not with Brumback's conclusions and forthwith applies his interpretation to the subject, intimating that Brumback's *scriptural base is inadequate*.[1] Anthony Hoekema also contends that his treatment of glossolalia is scripture based and correct. Referring to the charismatic experiences of Neo-Pentecostals he states: "Yet the primary question for us must always be, not what kind of experience a person has had, but what the Bible teaches. Experience must always be tested by Scripture, and not Scripture by experience."[2]

While Pentecostals would not totally disagree with that statement, they would insist that both Scripture and experience serve as validators of one another. Often experience occurs and then those involved search the Scriptures to see if there is a precedent for what has happened to them. This has happened to both classical Pentecostals and Charismatics. Which came first, Pentecost or the New Testament? This argument is silly, everyone knows it was Pentecost. The disciples were not enjoined by Jesus to wait until the New Testament came and then they could search the scriptures for understanding about what they were about to experience. Rather, Peter (Acts 2:14) announces to the gathering crowd: "Let me explain this to you . . ." In other words, allow me to enlighten you regarding this that we have *experienced*. The chicken or the egg argument just doesn't wash here. Jesus told the disciples what they were going to *experience*, as did the prophet Joel.[3] Peter appeals to scripture in his explanation of their experience, but that is not what Hoekema appears to mean when he appeals to the priority of scripture. He argues that all religious experience must be validated by scripture. Find it in the Bible first, then experience it.

HOLY SPIRIT BAPTISM OCCURS AT CONVERSION

Basic to an understanding of the Evangelical/Fundamentalist notion that Spirit-baptism occurs at conversion (or as some would affirm, at the moment of water baptism) is the belief that the new Christian receives all of God's spiritual blessing and provision at conversion. Once converted the

1. Millikin, *Testing Tongues*, 8.

2. Hoekema, *Holy Spirit Baptism*, 15.

3. See Joel 2:28–29.

person receives all that God intended relative to spiritual matters.[4] This idea is derived from their particular interpretation of the Pentecost event recorded in Acts. In Hoekema's words:

> We have seen so far that the expression "to be baptized in the Spirit" is used in the Gospels and in Acts 1:5 to designate the once for all, historical event of the outpouring of the Spirit on Pentecost day. In this sense the baptism of the Spirit is never repeated. In Acts 11:16, however, the expression "to be baptized in the Spirit" describes the reception of the Spirit for salvation by people who were not Christians before. In this sense the baptism of the Spirit can be repeated.[5]

Harold Lindsell, a traditionalist, does affirm a fullness of the Spirit subsequent to the initial indwelling at the new birth:

> All believers are sealed, indwelt, and experience the sanctifying grace of the Spirit in them. But no believer is, at the time of the new birth or even later, necessarily filled or controlled by the Holy Spirit. The filling of which we speak is certainly the believer's birthright. It belongs to him or her because he or she is a child of God and a joint heir with Jesus Christ. It is the Father's wish that all of His children be filled with the Spirit. It is a blessing that must be claimed.[6]

Though Lindsell does affirm this filling of the Spirit to be a post-conversion event, he does not affirm that the evidence of this filling is speaking in tongues. He maintains that outward evidences are not essential, since "nowhere does Scripture say that there is only one sign or confirmation marking the Spirit's fullness."[7]

The evidence, for Lindsell, is an intuitive *knowing* that one has received this fullness.[8] No visible evidential sign is needed in order for one to have received the fullness of the Spirit. "Faith," Lindsell says, "lays hold of the promise of God, embraces that promise, and believes that the answer has come, whether or not there is any outward visible sign."[9]

---

4. Dunn, *Baptism in the Holy Spirit*; see this work for a full treatment of the traditional view. For a critique of Dunn, see Ervin, *Conversion-Initiation*.

5. Hoekema, *Holy Spirit Baptism*, 20

6. Lindsell, *Holy Spirit*, 111.

7. Ibid., 121.

8. Ibid.

9. Ibid., 122.

It is apparent from Lindsell's comments above that there are those of the traditionalist persuasion who do view the fullness of the Spirit as a second or continuing work of grace. Overall, however, it seems evident that this is a minority view.

As shall be seen, the classical Pentecostal and the Neo-Pentecostal both affirm that this baptism is a post-conversion experience. Depending on their theological roots, it would be considered either a second work of grace or perhaps a third work of grace. And some would want to say that there is a continuing work of grace constantly at work in the believer's life. The manifestation of glossolalia is for the latter but a small part of that event. For most the expression of glossolalia would definitely be considered as *primary evidence* that such a baptism has occurred.

The traditionalist, on the other hand, viewing conversion and Spirit-baptism as synonymous, discounts charismatic gifts for the modern church and completely misunderstands the entire Pentecostal and Charismatic movements, calling it the *Tongues Movement*. Since, in their theology, all believers have already received the Holy Spirit in his fullness at conversion (or at infant or other water baptism), the contention is over the validity of speaking in tongues for the contemporary church. This, then, becomes the entire issue: *Is speaking in tongues valid for today?*

IS SPEAKING IN TONGUES VALID FOR TODAY?

It is the position of those who hold the traditional viewpoint that speaking in tongues by Christians today is neither desirable nor of value. This idea is based primarily upon their hermeneutical understanding of Paul's teaching in his first letter to the Corinthian church.

Hoekema contends:

> In the previous chapter we saw that Neo-Pentecostal teaching on "baptism in the Spirit" is not supported by Scripture, and therefore must be rejected. There is no Biblical basis for the view that every Christian must seek a "baptism in the Spirit" after his conversion in order to enjoy the totality of the Spirit's presence and the fullness of His power. If this is so, then the teaching that speaking with tongues—a spontaneous utterance of sounds in a language the speaker has never learned and does not understand—is either the indispensable or else highly desirable evidence that one has received the baptism in the Spirit is also rejected. For if the Neo-Pentecostal teaching about Spirit-baptism is wrong, it is obvious

that their teaching about the evidence of the "Spirit-baptism" must also be wrong.[10]

B. B. Warfield, a Presbyterian, argued that "the gifts were no longer required and that they belonged to a period of immaturity, of childish speaking which was to give way to maturity."[11] Because this was so, from Warfield's point of view, all modern claims to speaking in tongues "must be spurious, a dangerous combination of jargon and psychopathology, found only in the lunatic fringe of Christendom and possibly inspired by the Devil."[12] This notion that the gift of tongues was merely for an immature church is also embraced by Millikin. "Many scholars conclude from this that tongues must be regarded as a gift of God for the time of the church's infancy."[13]

Robert G. Gromacki postulates that contemporary expressions of glossolalia may be demonic, noting that "many conservatives believe that speaking in tongues ceased in the apostolic era and that any manifestation of the phenomenon since that time must be regarded as not only simulated counterfeit, but actually of Satanic origin."[14]

It would be a disservice to the traditionalist position to leave the impression that all of that persuasion consider speaking in tongues today to be Satanic. Millikin has said:

> In addition, our response to the tongues movement must not deny the possibility of experiencing the miraculous workings of God today. Some have sought totally to reject modern tongues-speaking on the basis that God intended for tongues, along with the other miracles, to cease after the apostolic age. Based strictly on biblical exegesis, this is a difficult position to maintain. In our evaluation of modern tongues-speaking the door must be left open for the sovereign Spirit to bestow the gift of tongues today (1 Cor 2:11).[15]

Though these allowances are made by some, most traditionalists hold a dim view of the practice of glossolalia. It is their opinion that the gift was frowned on by the Apostle Paul and given little value in his theology.

10. Hoekema, *Holy Spirit Baptism*, 32.

11. Quoted in Griffiths, *Three Men*, 35.

12. Ibid., 36.

13. Millikin, *Testing Tongues*, 31.

14. Gromacki, *Tongues Movement*, 46.

15. Millikin, *Testing Tongues*, 43.

Great weight is given to Paul's statement that it is better to prophesy than to speak in tongues, and ignoring the qualifying interpretation of tongues, they deduce that he gives this phenomenon a lesser value than the other. Referring to 1 Corinthians 12, 13, and 14, Hoekema observes:

> According to these chapters, then—the only chapters where speaking with tongues is discussed in detail—tongue-speaking has limited value. In fact, only two uses of tongue-speaking are described in 1 Corinthians 14: a limited use in church assemblies, and a use for personal edification. We note, then, that according to Paul's teaching here tongue-speaking is of some value for one's own edification. Yet even this value must be judged on the basis of Scripture to be a limited one.[16]

Gromacki comments, in reference to 1 Corinthians 12:28, "Here tongues is placed last and regarded as the least of gifts, although it must be recognized as a gift and an essential part of the body of Christ at that time."[17]

The deductions made by the traditionalist regarding the practice of glossolalia today are usually based upon their *particular* interpretation of certain passages of Scripture. They examine the following Scriptures: Acts 2:1–42, 8:4–24, 9:1–10, 10:1–48, 19:1–7, 1 Corinthians 12, 13, 14. These certainly are the vital New Testament passages dealing with the matter of glossolalia; however, it seems apparent that the traditionalists are not totally forthright, and in order to lend support to their position they ignore pertinent material, explain away difficult areas, or dismiss them lightly.

A SUMMARY

In summation, the traditionalist position regarding glossolalia in the modern church affirms that the new believer receives the totality of the Spirit at conversion. The gift of tongues was a valid expression for the early church but was given only to that immature body until it reached maturity. Therefore, it is no longer needed by today's modern, mature church. While it was a valid gift it held little value or importance for the early church.

Several questions should be posed here at the end of this chapter:

---

16. Hoekema, *Holy Spirit Baptism*, 50–51.
17. Gromacki, *Tongues Movement*, 119.

First, was the experience of those first Christians due to the New Testament or does the existence of the New Testament issue out of the experience of that first community of believers?

To assume that God will only reveal himself through the written record is untenable. Scripture itself informs us that God has primarily revealed himself through his Son, our Lord Jesus Christ.

It is still through the body of his Son, the church, that he continues to reveal himself to humanity. That revelation will not do violence to an open-ended method of interpretation of Scripture, nor will it be inconsistent with Scripture. It will prevent man from locking God in the box of someone's particular dogma.

Moving, then, from the premise questioned above, we see the traditionalist deals with glossolalia in a like manner. There is the implication that the scriptures were written first, prior to the Christian experience of the charismatic gifts, particularly glossolalia. We must understand that however much *we* do, the scriptures do not treat the charismata propositionally.

Second, is the modern church really mature? With all of the divisions in the church today it seems to resemble the infantile Corinthian church more than the hoary head of maturity.

Third, if the gift of tongues was given to an immature church and dispensed with when that church arrived at some point of maturity, surely it must have been of much more value for spiritual growth than the traditionalist wants to acknowledge. The two arguments tend to cancel each other. Perhaps John Haughey is correct in this observation:

> Many claim to see a "new age of the Spirit" dawning in our midst. For those who do not, one could argue, on the basis of the needs of the contemporary Church and culture, that it would be good if a new age of the Spirit did dawn on us, since so many of the functions theologically associated with the Spirit seem to be required more urgently than ever to meet those needs.[18]

The classical Pentecostal would say a hearty *Amen* to that, acknowledging the dependence the church has upon the Holy Spirit to fulfill its mission on the earth. The traditionalist position and that of the Pentecostals and Charismatics stand poles apart in many respects.

---

18. Haughey, *Conspiracy*, 118–19.

5

The Classical Pentecostal Position

To assume that within Pentecostal ranks there is a unity of doctrinal viewpoint would be to ignore the diversity that God has built
into the church. There is a broad spectrum represented in that movement.
Two of the larger Pentecostal denominations are the Assemblies of God,
hereinafter identified as A/G, and the Church of God (Cleveland, TN),
hereinafter identified as CGCT. Since these groups of the Pentecostal
family tend to be representative, we will work primarily with their positions regarding classical Pentecostalism's stance on glossolalia.

PENTECOSTAL FUNDAMENTALISTS?

A brief glance at the classical Pentecostals could cause one to assume that
they were inherently Fundamentalist in their faith. That conclusion can
only be made from a cursory review of their theology. The astute scholar
would find that they are actually more at home in the Evangelical camp
than anywhere. (It is true that some segments of the movement are definitely Fundamentalist in their theological orientation. Also, some individuals within the denominations that are essentially Evangelical would
have to be classed as Fundamentalist.)

Far from standing in the tradition of B. B. Warfield, et al. (although
they do hold the Bible to be the inspired Word of God and the rule of
faith and practice), they do not affirm that it is only through the Bible
that God reveals himself to the church. They would view the church to
be a historic faith, but they would not relegate the activity of God to past
history, insisting, rather, that he continues to reveal himself in contemporary human culture through the church. Faith for them is more than an
intellectual exercise, endorsing a set of propositional doctrines or creedal
statements. It is a living, active experience alive with the *immanence* of

God. Though God did act historically at the cross, at the garden tomb, and on the day of Pentecost, he did not consummate all of his activity at those points of history, expecting that the results would be passed on routinely from one generation to the next. It is their contention that God has no grandchildren. That God desires to confront each succeeding generation with his person, his purpose, his provision, his plan, and his power is a given in their theology.

Pentecostals believe that God continues to speak to the church today in fresh and creative ways. He speaks through the preached Word; he speaks through prophetic utterance; he also speaks through the gift of tongues and the interpretation of tongues, which are viewed as the equivalent of prophecy. Also, he speaks in that *still small voice* in the heart.

It would seem, therefore, that classical Pentecostals do not fall into the Fundamentalist circle, since they embrace and expect the miraculous acts of God to occur in today's world by the power of the Holy Spirit They also believe that God continues to speak to the church, revealing himself through the charismatic gifts of the Spirit.

PENTECOSTAL PRESUPPOSITIONS

The classical Pentecostal brings several presuppositions to the subject of glossolalia. First, the quality of Christian living, in general, is not today what it was in the time of the early church. Secondly, the modern church is woefully lacking in spiritual maturity and power and does need and will continue to need the charismatic gifts of the Holy Spirit.

Pentecostals also believe that their particular interpretation of Scripture is the only accurate approach to the subject of glossolalia. Because of their view regarding the Baptism with the Holy Spirit, the matter of speaking in tongues is not an issue in itself, simply a part of a larger whole.

Much of the doctrinal stance of Pentecostals on this matter is inherited from R. A. Torrey, et al. Much of the language employed theologically by Pentecostals can be traced back to these roots. Torrey, in his work on Spirit-baptism, sets forth five statements as his premise concerning Spirit-baptism:

1. There are a number of designations in the Bible for this one experience.
2. The baptism of the Holy Spirit is a definite experience.

3. The baptism of the Holy Spirit is separate from and distinct from his regenerating work.

4. The baptism with the Holy Spirit is always connected with testimony and service.

5. The baptism with the Holy Spirit imparts power—power for service.[1]

The language employed above by Torrey is certainly reflected in the language of Pentecostals, as anyone familiar with Pentecostals will concur. The meaning of some of the terms as used by Pentecostals will be different from Torrey's usage, but some will be the same.

HOLY SPIRIT BAPTISM: A POST-CONVERSION EXPERIENCE

While classical Pentecostals would want to affirm the uniqueness of Pentecost day, they would not agree with the traditionalist that it was an unrepeatable event. Nor would they concur that the fullness of the Spirit comes at the moment of conversion. Myer Pearlman (A/G) states their position:

> God is always and necessarily present everywhere; in Him all men live, move and have their being. But indwelling means that He is present in a new way, sustaining a "personal" relationship to the individual. This union with God, which is called indwelling, is produced in reality by the presence of the whole Trinity. . . . But since it is the special ministry of the Holy Spirit to indwell the hearts of men, the experience is commonly known as the indwelling of the Holy Sprit. It is believed by many orthodox scholars that God imparted to Adam, not only physical and mental life, but also the indwelling Spirit, which he lost because of sin, not only for himself but also for his descendants. This absence of the Spirit has left man in spiritual darkness and weakness.[2]

P. C. Nelson expresses the thought in this manner: "The Father draws the sinner (John 6:44); the Holy Spirit convicts the sinner (John 16:8), and the sinner is regenerated by the power of the Spirit—is "born of the Spirit"; "born again" (John 1:11–13; 3:3–7)."[3]

---

1. Torrey, *Baptism*, 3–20.

2. Pearlman, *Doctrines of the Bible*, 306.

3. Nelson, *Bible Doctrines*, 55.

This indwelling addressed by Pearlman and Nelson is the initial work of the Holy Spirit in the salvific history of an individual. This is the new birth.

Pearlman contends further:

> By faith and repentance man turns to God and becomes regenerated. Regeneration by the Spirit involves a union with God and Christ (1 Cor 6:17) which is known as indwelling. 1 Corinthians 6:19. This indwelling or possession of the Spirit is the mark of a New Testament Christian. In regeneration the Holy Spirit effects a radical change in the soul by imparting a new principle of life. But this does not imply that the child of God is at once perfect. There remain inherited and acquired weaknesses; there are still the world, the flesh, and the devil to overcome.[4]

It is the classical Pentecostal's belief that once born again there is still work for the Spirit to do in the life of the new believer. That is bringing the new babe in Christ to maturity. This is a progressive process and is called sanctification.[5] Those who affirm progressive sanctification believe that it occurs throughout a believer's lifetime.

A third aspect of the Spirit's ministry to the believer is his energizing work. Pentecostals believe that this comes to us in the baptism with the Holy Spirit and that its purpose is to empower one for holy living and service. Pearlman argues:

> This last phase of the Spirit's work is set forth in Christ's promise: "But ye shall receive power, after that the Holy Ghost is come upon you: and ye shall be witnesses unto me." Acts 1:8. The main feature of this promise is power for service and not regeneration for eternal life. Whenever we read of the Spirit coming upon, resting upon, falling upon, or filling people, the reference is never to the saving work of the Spirit but always to power for service.[6]

---

4. Pearlman, *Doctrines of the Bible*, 307–8.

5. Not all Pentecostals would endorse the idea of progressive sanctification. The Church of God (Cleveland, TN), affirms a second definite work of grace in sanctification. This occurs prior to Spirit-baptism and is prerequisite to that baptism. Other smaller Pentecostal groups would concur with that position. Pentecostal denominations were formed from two primary sources. David Faupel observes that one rises out of the Holiness Movement and the other out of the Keswick group. The Assemblies of God derives its primary roots from the Keswick group, while the Church of God finds its spiritual heritage in the Holiness Movement (Faupel *American,* 20).

6. Pearlman, *Doctrines of the Bible,* 309.

Nelson argues:

> All believers are entitled to, and should ardently expect, and earnestly seek, the promise of the Father, the Baptism in the Holy Ghost and fire, according to the command of our Lord Jesus Christ. This was the normal experience of the early Christian Church. With it come the enduement of power for life and service. . . . This wonderful experience is distinct from and subsequent to the experience of the new birth.[7]

Charles W. Conn (CGCT) comments on the empowerment of the Spirit: "He empowers, arouses our energies, stiffens our moral fiber. He is power. . . . Men can be invigorated, soul and mind, until their power cannot be fathomed or equaled or subdued."[8]

Using the exact same scriptures the traditionalists use to disprove the validity of Spirit-baptism accompanied by glossolalia, the classical Pentecostals affirm what they consider to be an accurate interpretation of scripture in order to provide a biblical basis for this new life in Christ, which also includes the dimension of the Pentecostal experience.

It is the classical Pentecostal position that accompanying the baptism with the Spirit will be the charisms of the Spirit. On the whole, no Pentecostal, classical or Neo, would limit the gifts of the Spirit to glossolalia alone. Wade H. Horton (CGCT) refutes the notion that Pentecostals are "hung-up" on tongues: "We did not, and still do not, place as much importance on glossolalia itself as some do today or as much as others claim we do. We are, however, without question unshakably convinced that glossolalia is a scriptural phenomenon that has its proper place in both private and public worship."[9]

IS SPEAKING IN TONGUES VALID FOR TODAY?

Classical Pentecostals affirm the validity of tongues-speech for today; that is a given. Pearlman (A/G), Nelson (A/G), Horton (CGCT), and Conn (CGCT) all endorse this phenomenon.[10] Pearlman appeals to theologians from the historic churches for support in his conclusions, citing G.

---

7. Nelson, *Bible Doctrines*, 77.

8. Conn, *Pillars of Pentecost*, 85–86.

9. Horton, *Glossolalia Phenomenon*, 16.

10. Nelson, *Bible Doctrines*, 91; Pearlman, *Doctrines of the Bible*, 313–314; Horton, *Glossolalia Phenomenon*, 35.

B. Stevens of Yale and A. B. MacDonald, a Scotch Presbyterian minister, emphasizing that his is not a private interpretation.[11]

Charles Conn notes that "In the Scriptures the Baptism with the Holy Ghost was always attended by conspicuous manifestations of the Divine Presence. The common manifestation was speaking with unknown tongues, or languages. This phenomenon was consistent evidence that the Holy Spirit had come . . . Tongues gave immediate witness that the Spirit had come. Speaking in tongues is therefore appropriately called the initial evidence of the Baptism with the Holy Spirit."[12]

It is probably this affirmation more than any other issue that brings Pentecostal theology into the arena of controversy. For the classical, the initial physical evidence for Spirit-baptism is the indispensable proof of speaking in tongues. On the whole they are adamant about that.

There are, however, Pentecostal scholars who would affirm that tongues may be an evidence but not the only evidence. And such Pentecostal pioneers as T. B. Barratt and George Jeffreys did not embrace the American notion of the initial evidence doctrine.[13]

11. Pearlman, *Doctrines of the Bible*, 314.

12. Horton, *Glossolalia Phenomenon*, 35.

13. Spittler, *Perspectives*, 68; see also Barratt, *Latter Rain*, 152.

6

The Neo-Pentecostal Position

A<small>N ENCOUNTER WITH THE</small> Neo-Pentecostal position brings one to a broad spectrum of theological thought. For the Neo position contains a conglomeration of persons with varied theological backgrounds. To present a position as representative would possibly be stretching the meaning of the word. However, that is what I shall endeavor to do here. In attempting to do that I will draw upon a variety of writers, both Catholic and Protestant. The Neo-Pentecostal also brings the baggage of his or her background to this subject. I will not attempt to cover those ramifications here, since they are too varied to attempt to standardize. Suffice it to say that the reader should be cognizant that the composite experience of any given writer influences that person's conclusions. Following the pattern established in the two previous chapters, I will analyze Neo-Pentecostals' views of what constitutes Spirit-baptism and their viewpoint on the validity of tongues-speech for our day.

HOLY SPIRIT BAPTISM:
A POST-CONVERSION EXPERIENCE?

As one observes the development of Neo-Pentecostal thought, one becomes aware that, although many differences remain, there are many similarities between the Neo and the Classical positions. One similarity is the concurrence that Spirit-baptism is a post-conversion experience. Presbyterian scholar J. Rodman Williams, a Neo-Pentecostal who has drunk deeply at the fountain of Reformed theology, affirms that Spirit-baptism is experienced subsequent to the new birth:

> Pentecost represents more than a once-for-all incident in the life of the early church. The Spirit was not poured out upon the community of faith on that first day to remain therein until the end of

time. However, the event itself is not always coincidental with the inception of faith; it may occur then or at a later time. In fact many would testify to "baptism with the Spirit" as happening somewhere along the way of faith, not at the beginning. Others would attest that this experience occurred at the first moment of faith. But the usual witness is the former, namely, that there has been belief some time before the Pentecostal event took place.[1]

It is interesting that a man of the theological stature of Williams, coming from the Reformed tradition, can make the above affirmations. He, in fact, repudiates the traditional Reformed view of Spirit-baptism being a co-conversion event. For him, it is post-conversion, though he allows for co-conversion. Speaking of the traditionalists' viewpoint, Williams comments, "There is little recognition of 'baptism with the Spirit' as referring to a further action of God which is the particular work of the Holy Spirit."[2]

Larry Christenson, a Charismatic Lutheran scholar, is quite explicit when he avers, "beyond conversion, beyond the assurance of salvation, beyond having the Holy Spirit, there is a baptism with the Holy Spirit."[3] Christenson continues the thought: "But one thing is constant in the Scripture, and it is most important: It is never merely assumed that a person has been baptized with the Holy Spirit. When he has been baptized with the Holy Spirit the person knows it. It is a definite experience."[4]

Dennis Bennett, a Charismatic Episcopalian, differentiates between the two events, understanding that conversion is the event whereby we are baptized into Christ by the Holy Spirit and the pentecostal event the baptism of the believer into the Holy Spirit by Jesus. Hence, he states, "Notice clearly, however, that baptism with water is the outward sign of baptism into Jesus (salvation) (1 Cor 12:13), but not the baptism by Jesus into the Holy Spirit (Pentecost) (Luke 3:16)."[5] (This idea is much like that of some classical Pentecostals and may have been borrowed from them.)

An amplification of the above statement is found later in Bennett's treatment of the subject. Here he would affirm:

1. Williams, *Pentecostal Reality*, 15.
2. Ibid., 21.
3. Christenson, *Speaking in Tongues*, 37.
4. Ibid., 38.
5. Bennett, *Holy Spirit*, 26.

> The Holy Spirit comes to live in us when we receive Jesus, and are born again of the Spirit. The baptism in the Holy Spirit is the pouring out of the Spirit. We cannot very well expect Him to pour out through us until He is living in us, so before we ask to be baptized in the Holy Spirit, we must first be sure that we have indeed received the Lord Jesus as Savior, and invited Him to live in us by His Spirit.[6]

One can conclude from these statements that Bennett believes that Spirit-baptism occurs subsequent to regeneration.

Through his perusal of the five incidents of Spirit-baptism in the book of Acts, Don Basham (Disciples of Christ) concludes that the pentecostal event is an experience separate from and following the conversion of the believer: "From an examination of all five accounts we see the same truth emerging—that conversion is one experience and the baptism in the Holy Spirit is a second, subsequent experience."[7]

It becomes apparent that the preponderance of Neo-Pentecostal thought appears to affirm the separation of the conversion experience from the pentecostal event in a person's life. Spirit- baptism is, then, for most Neo-Pentecostals, a post-conversion experience.

IS SPEAKING IN TONGUES VALID FOR TODAY?

Here again, for the most part, the Neo-Pentecostal would stand with the classical Pentecostal in affirming an answer to the above question. Glossolalia is not only valid for today but is viewed as an integral part of the design of God to bring power and authority to the proclamation of the gospel through the ordained ministry and the lives of the laity. Like their classical counterparts, Neo-Pentecostals do not isolate tongues-speech to the detriment of the other charisms. The baptism with the Holy Spirit brings to the believer the availability of all the gifts of the Spirit. All of the gifts are of equal value for the church, and the Spirit dispenses them as he wills. The gifts are given for the benefit of the entire church, though they do bring profit to the individual through whom the gifts are dispensed.

---

6. Ibid., 36.

7. Basham, *Ministering the Baptism,* 19.

Speaking of the charismatic gifts in general, which would include glossolalia, Donald Bloesch, an Evangelical Reformed theologian, calls for an openness on the part of the church toward the recovery of those gifts.[8]

> If we are to have spiritual renewal in our time, the church must be open again to the special gifts and charisms given by the Spirit of God for the purpose of ministry in the world.
>   . . . When these gifts are in the hands of those who stand solidly on the Scriptural revelation and who seek to use them in the service of Christ, they can be of immense aid to the church in its ministry of reconciliation and redemption. Christianity is after all not only an institutional religion but also a charismatic religion.[9]

Bloesch affirms the validity and value of glossolalia; however, he would not go as far as some classical and Neo-Pentecostals who regard speaking in tongues as a sign or evidence of having been filled with the Spirit. This reflects his Reformed view regarding Spirit-baptism, that view being that the believer receives the totality of the Spirit at the point of regeneration and not subsequent to the new birth. For Bloesch, this is simply a manifestation of the presence of the Holy Spirit already resident in the believer. He also affirms with the traditionalist that the instruction of Paul minimizes the value of glossolalia, viewing this gift of the Spirit as something needful only for children in the faith. Bloesch contends that "speaking in tongues is a crutch or psychic aid that can occasionally benefit even some who are more spiritually advanced, although it more appropriately belongs to the childhood of faith."[10]

Bloesch's position with regard to the place and value of tongues-speech is disturbing on two counts. First, it tends to weaken his appeal to the Church for an openness to the charisms of the Spirit by taking the traditionalist view of the value of tongues. It is only one step from there to the deprecation of any one of the gifts. The view of Paul was not to deprecate any one of the gifts, but to bring balance in their manifestation. (Admittedly, Paul does indicate in his first letter to the Corinthians that prophecy is more productive for believers than is uninterpreted tongues;

---

8. Bloesch's comments are included here, even though he would not consider himself to be part of the Neo-Pentecostal movement; according to this writer's past information, he does not speak in tongues. His clear and persuasive argument in favor of the charisms of the Spirit demand inclusion here.

9. Bloesch, *Reform*, 114.

10. Ibid., 116.

however, this must not be construed to mean that he devalues glossolalia.) Secondly (though I doubt this is his intent), what he states could be taken as an inference of spiritual elitism: those who do practice speaking in tongues may be immature, while those who do not are the more mature. It is true that there are some Pentecostals, Neo and classical, who express the same thought from their perspective. Those who do not speak in tongues are immature and those who do are not. Both of these ideas are to be rejected, for they can become seeds of division in the church.

Lutheran theologian Larry Christenson is of the opinion that one should never merely assume that a person has received the baptism with the Holy Spirit. For him it is an event. A part of that event is the manifestation of the Spirit in the form of glossolalia, though he would not affirm that it always has to be that way. "Is speaking in tongues the only valid objective manifestation that a person has had this definite, instantaneous experience of the baptism with the Holy Spirit? Scripture does not say that it is the only one. But in showing us the pattern, Scripture gives us no consistent suggestion of any other."[11]

For Christenson, it is not so much that one has to speak in tongues to be baptized in the Holy Spirit but that one who receives the gift of the fullness of the Spirit may also receive from the Holy Spirit the gift of speaking in tongues. He speaks of this gift as a further blessing and a further power.[12]

Christenson rightly identifies the point here: "The central issue in the Book of Acts is not speaking in tongues, but this deeper issue of the baptism with the Holy Spirit."[13] If this pentecostal event is valid, so are the accompanying manifestations of that event.

Basham expresses his viewpoint, observing, "We cannot dogmatically say that everyone must speak in tongues in order to have the baptism, we merely point out that it is the normative experience."[14] Bennett takes a more dogmatic stance when he states: "Can I receive the Holy Spirit without speaking in tongues? It comes with the package! Speaking in tongues

11. Christenson, *Tongues*, 54.

12. Ibid., 57.

13. Ibid.

14. Basham, *Handbook on Tongues*, 34.

is not the baptism in the Holy Spirit, but it is what happens when and as you are baptized in the Spirit."[15]

From the statements of these authors we can conclude, for their part at least, the Neo-Pentecostal position would be to affirm the validity of glossolalia for the Church in our day. They would not say that it has to occur in the pentecostal event but that it probably will. As to the value of the gift of tongues, most Neo-Pentecostals agree: It deepens one's prayer life and effectiveness in prayer. It is edifying for the person exercising the gift. It strengthens them in spirit, soul, and body. It offers a new dimension in worship of God. Provided that it is interpreted, it edifies the Christian community when exercised in public meetings.

The benefits derived in the first three instances should encourage seeking Christians to open their lives to this gift of the Spirit. In all of these areas, even the wisest among us are deficient. Could it be that insipid religion might become an effervescent faith through the practice of this gift? The Neo-Pentecostal would affirm a resounding, It can!

To the above considerations of Protestant writers we would add the comments of Roman Catholic Jesuit Donald Gelpi. It is his opinion that speaking in tongues has value in that, like the other gifts, its generic purpose is to render man more docile to the Spirit of Christ and hence more like Jesus, the Spirit-filled Messiah. But like all the gifts, glossolalia also has an ecclesial purpose as well. It serves to remind the worshiping community of the first Pentecost in which the Spirit of Christ was poured out upon men as a seal of God's new, spiritual covenant. In its use and cultivation, glossolalia like all the gifts must be regulated by the law of love, interpreted by faith, and nourished by hope.[16]

A SUMMARY

In summary, the Neo-Pentecostal would affirm, along with his classical Pentecostal brethren, that the pentecostal event, Spirit-baptism, is subsequent to the conversion experience. Accompanying this baptism, normally but not necessarily, will be the manifestation of speaking in tongues. It is a valid expression of the Spirit in the church today—not only for the individual believer, but for the entire Christian community, both directly and indirectly. All of this is concluded by a search of and interpretation of the

15. Bennett, *Holy Spirit and You*, 64.

16. Gelpi, *Pentecostalism*, 145.

same scriptures perused by the traditionalist and the classical Pentecostal. The Neo-Pentecostal, as does the Classical, appeals to the scriptures to confirm the validity of that which, in reality, has been experienced. It is their opinion that they stand on firm ground.

History has shown us that when glossolalia is exercised within the framework of pastoral discipline, wisdom, and a spirit of love, it produces in the life of the church the continuing power of the Holy Spirit to fulfill the mission of our Lord Jesus Christ. This has been true in both the Charismatic movement and the Pentecostal movement.

PART THREE

The Normative Argument

7

Considerations in Pentecostal Hermeneutics

IN ORDER TO BUILD a base of understanding for our current subject it is necessary to consider two theological concepts that have direct bearing on the matter of hermeneutics: general revelation and special revelation. Both address the epistemological question of knowledge of God, as well as the ontological issues involved. Special revelation is our main interest relative to Pentecostal hermeneutics.

General revelation has to do with the disclosure of God in creation. As Paul insists in the first chapter of the epistle to the church at Rome, God has made himself known in creation, and only those who refuse to see fail to see him. Humanity discovers, through search and investigation, a knowledge of God embedded in the creation. All truth is God's truth, therefore any matter that proves to actually be true is the truth of God. According to T. F. Torrance, human discovery of "the universe which God has made, and made to be one, and which he means us to explore and progressively to bring to faithful expression in appropriate sciences" is the heart of general revelation.[1] General revelation serves as a natural catalyst intended to bring mankind to a consciousness of God.

Bruce Demarest, an evangelical scholar, has noted:

> Historically, Christian theology has differentiated between general and special revelation, both as to content and focus. General revelation, mediated through nature, conscience, and the providential ordering of history, traditionally has been understood as a universal witness to God's existence and character. Through the modalities of general revelation, man at large knows both that there is a God and in broad outline what He is like.[2]

1. Torrance, *Reality*, 10.
2. Demarest, *General Revelation*, 14.

(By "broad outline" Demarest means that we can know about God, in a general sense.)

Karl Barth refers to this idea as God's biography. God reveals enough about himself through created things that mankind can know he is there. To know God exhaustively is beyond the scope of human possibility, therefore, God allows man to perceive only as much knowledge of God as man can cope with.

Torrance has observed, "Now since God has endowed his creation with a rationality and beauty of its own in created correspondence to his transcendent rationality and beauty, the more the created universe unfolds its marvelous symmetries and harmonies to our scientific inquiries, the more it is bound to fulfill its role as a theater which reflects the glory of the Creator and resounds to his praise."[3]

Special revelation moves beyond general revelation in that God reveals specific details about himself to a specific people for a specific purpose. The difference lies between knowing *about* God in a general way, that is, the creative acts of God, and knowing the person of God in an intimate, personal relationship.

The concept of special revelation embodies the idea of God revealing himself in a particular and significant manner. This includes his dealings with mankind—Israel in particular—through the medium of christophanies, the burning bush, his prophets, the oral tradition, and the written record found in the writings of the Old Testament. Special revelation in the New Testament comes through the incarnate Son, the oral tradition, the gospel records, the various epistles, and the Revelation. All of these comprise the body of special revelation that has been historically perceived to be a body of revelation that is complete and cannot be altered or added to. Demarest notes:

> Here Christian orthodoxy has insisted that answers to life's profoundest questions—the secret nature of God and His will for man—are provided by a supernatural revelatory disclosure to a special people. Through the modalities of God's mighty acts in history, the teachings and deeds of Jesus Christ, and the writing of the Bible, the divine salvific plan is unveiled to a particular people.[4]

3. Torrance, *Reality,* 10–11.

4. Demarest, *General Revelation,* 14.

A PARTICULAR PENTECOSTAL HERMENEUTIC?

It is this latter body of revealed truth that must be considered in regard to the concept of a unique Pentecostal hermeneutic. Can there be a unique hermeneutic of special revelation that can be especially termed *Pentecostal?* Does the uniqueness of the Pentecostal movement demand a particular hermeneutic in order to maintain that uniqueness? Is the Pentecostal movement, and Pentecostal theology in particular, such a special part of the Christian Church that it must develop a hermeneutic exclusively its own? There are some who believe that a Pentecostal hermeneutic is a primary concern for modern Pentecostal theologians. It will be the task of this chapter to determine whether such a concern is valid and to demonstrate that any Pentecostal hermeneutic that might emerge must rise out of the historic church's hermeneutical praxis. Also, my concern here will be to offer some direction in hermeneutical considerations for Pentecostals in our approach to Holy Scripture, its interpretation, and the construction of theological concepts or doctrine, especially in relation to the initial evidence doctrine.

The call for a special Pentecostal hermeneutic usually is based upon the idea that modern day Pentecostals are the recipients of *special revelation* that extends beyond the body of special revelation considered above. In order to maintain clarity and avoid confusion, this extension of special revelation shall hereafter be referred to as *extra-revelation.* Extra-revelation emerges from the charismatic expressions of the Holy Spirit revealed in Pentecostalism in the form of prophecy, the gift of tongues, the gift of interpretation, the word of knowledge and the word of wisdom. Also, the supernatural expressions of miracles and healings would be included with the foregoing, since they are considered continuing self-disclosure on God's part.

Mark McLean (A/G), who has called for a particular *Pentecostal* hermeneutic, argues:

> It is my contention that not only is a Pentecostal hermeneutic a vital necessity, if we are to have an effective ministry to our "modern" world, it is inescapable. A Pentecostal hermeneutic will either be well articulated, canonically based expression of normative Christianity, or the twentieth century Pentecostal movements will wither after the deaths of their charismatic leaders and become the religious oddities discussed in the opening chapters of future

books.... If we lose our hold on the Bible, that infallible rule of our faith, and conduct, we are lost.[5]

I share that concern; however, I also am concerned about the shape such a hermeneutic might take. History bears powerful witness to the results evoked by those who resort to special pleading for their particular approach to hermeneutical questions. The Montanists were a second-century charismatic movement within the church popularly known as the *New Prophecy* and were addicted to charismatic prophetic utterance. They claimed the right to a peculiar hermeneutical methodology, insisting that the prophetic utterance of the *Paraclete* (the inspired prophet) provided them with *revelation* from God that superseded the written word and made that word subject to the interpretation of the prophet. Montanists believed the Holy Spirit revealed to them the *true meaning* of the written word.[6]

Eric Nestler has noted that for the Montanists, charismatic prophetic experiences were the dynamo. They brought about the new teachings. In order to harmonize the new doctrines with the Bible, a tremendous amount of *rationalization* had to be invested. Out of this a new biblical hermeneutic was construed.[7]

This hermeneutical approach sounds familiar in some parts of the present day Pentecostal and Charismatic movements. The current popular notions of a *rhema* word[8] from God and the prosperity doctrine usu-

---

5. McLean, "Hermeneutic," 36.

6. Nestler, "Heresy," 67–75.

7. Ibid., 68.

8. The concept referred to here is that God speaks a *now* word to an individual that provides that person with a *new* understanding of a particular scripture verse or passage. As noted, this is highly subjective and leaves the discipline of hermeneutics completely out of the matter of biblical interpretation. Those who advocate this approach to Scripture invest the Greek word *rhema* with a meaning that cannot be supported in any sense of the word. The idea is set forth that *rhema* has a different meaning from the Greek term *logos*. *Rhema*, however, is merely another Greek word used in biblical times to mean *word*. God spoke through his Son, the eternal *Logos*, but now he speaks directly to an individual through this *rhema*, a fresh and new word. An accurate study of the two terms will show that such is not the case. The Holy Spirit does not contradict himself, meaning one thing when he inspired the writer to select a particular word with the meaning it held in that day and then investing it with another meaning for our day. Though John did give the term *logos* a meaning that was foreign to contemporary Greek usage, he did so in an attempt to impress upon his readers that Jesus is the *Logos*, the ultimate of all things, an idea popular with Greek thinking in that day. John did this under the impulse

ally violate many hermeneutical principles held by the historic church and place extra-revelation above the word of God in the sense that those who have received this extra-revelation possess a *deeper* understanding of what the Holy Spirit actually meant in that particular passage of scripture. This is usually arrived at hyper-subjectively with little, if any, proper hermeneutical labor involved. They too may resort to special pleading in their approach to the interpretation of scripture, as did the Montanists. It was this insistence upon extra-revelation that could stand above sound hermeneutical practice that led to the *Jesus Only* and *Latter Rain* aberrations in the Pentecostal movement and has led to similar aberrations in the Charismatic movement (for example, the distortion of the *Discipleship* doctrine and the *Shepherding* movement that it produced).

If the call for a hermeneutic that is particularly Pentecostal means that we set aside interpretive principles that have stood the test of time throughout the history of the church, we must rigorously resist such a notion. (In fairness to McLean, I must acknowledge that he does insist that there cannot be a *total* rejection of the hermeneutical tools of our evangelical heritage.)[9] A valid Pentecostal hermeneutic, one that is faithful to tradition, the revelation of God through Jesus Christ, and the accepted canon, must be one that rises out of the centuries of hermeneutical struggles of the historic church. Let us learn the lessons of history.

I suspect that there may be couched in the call for a special hermeneutic for Pentecostal theology the notion that God began something unique in the church when he birthed the modern Pentecostal movement. McLean's statement that the Pentecostal movement's "broad confessional statements are vital if the Pentecostal movements are to retain their self-identity and remain faithful to their task"[10] appears to invoke such an idea.

Should this be the case, we are treading on unstable ground. The Pentecostal movement must acknowledge its intrinsic unity with the historic church and not consider itself unique, in the sense that God *began* something *different* in the outpouring of his Spirit in the twentieth century. What God has accomplished through the Pentecostal movement is

---

of the Spirit in a special and particular way that is limited to the work of the Holy Spirit in inspiring the biblical writers as he formed the biblical canon. Twentieth-century believers cannot claim to possess that type of inspiration. The church has historically resisted those who have made such claims and were correct in so doing.

9. McLean, "Hermeneutic," 49.

10. Ibid., 38.

the restoration of an awareness of the person and work of the Holy Spirit to the larger church. It was the Pentecostal movement's witness to the contemporaneity of the acts of the Holy Spirit and His immanence in the lives of present day believers which evoked the birth of the Charismatic movement, a movement which has pervaded every part of the Christian Church in the twentieth century, both Protestant and Catholic, around the world. For this we should rejoice! Yet, in rejoicing, we must acknowledge that we are but a part of that great stream of salvific history. Do we really have a self identity and a task apart from the identity and task that belongs to the church universal, in heaven and on earth?

We Pentecostals are *not special* in the sense of privilege or uniqueness. God has not made a *special covenant* with us. We operate under the same covenant that is incumbent upon every part of the Christian church. Our specialness is only in the sense of responsibility—faithful witness to the immanence of the Spirit in the life of the modern church. Should it ever be that we Pentecostals fail to affirm that fact by the witness of our lives and the impact of our ministry, in addition to our theological witness, there will be no distinction about us whatever. Donald McGavran has noted the Pentecostal affirmation ". . . that God himself, through the Holy Spirit, personally guides and directs each disciple of Christ . . ." and that this ". . . principle of spontaneous action under the control of the spirit of Jesus as revealed in the Scriptures lies at the heart of the Pentecostal faith." It is this, declares McGavran, that has been the Pentecostals' prominent contribution to the larger church.[11]

Should we modern day Pentecostals lose sight of that contribution, all that has transpired over the years since the advent of modern Pentecost will simply pass into the historical record as one more flash in the pan, another Montanist movement or another Irvingite phenomenon. All of our theologizing about the Spirit's power for holy living and service will be a mere smudge on the pages of history. We are unique in the same sense that the larger church is unique. We are an integral part of that worldwide body of God's people, a body of people in whom the Spirit of God dwells, a body through whom the Holy Spirit desires to manifest Christ in all of his fullness, power and glory. Therefore, we must pray not only for the fullness of the Spirit for our Pentecostal fellowships but that the larger church might know that fullness as well. God has not abandoned that part

11. McGavran, *Church Growth*, 119–20.

of the church that is not pentecostal or charismatic in practice. He desires to make his people one in the Spirit! There is one Lord, there is one Spirit, and there is one body. That is irrevocable.

My suspicion is that our insistence on *distinctives* borders more on apologetics than hermeneutics. This may be true, since much of Pentecostal doctrine was formulated from a need to *defend* our experience of the Spirit rather than explain it. The attacks of the established churches upon the Pentecostal way evoked much of the theological work in those early days. It is true that initially our progenitors in the movement were busy seeking to understand, biblically, what had happened to them. However, a perusal of our history reveals to us that a great deal of labor was invested in apologetics designed to defend the Pentecostal way from the concerted attacks of those who would deny its reality. I believe that if viewed perceptively, it would become clear that the initial evidence doctrine, as an official Pentecostal *distinctive,* grew out of such apologetic endeavors.

Having stated the above, we Pentecostals must recognize that the hermeneutical struggle we are engaged in is a product not of our making. The evangelical community has posited that the book on special revelation closed with the passing of the last apostle. The Holy Spirit went on sabbatical. And maybe for them he has. But for those who continue to witness the Spirit at work, manifesting his gifts in the congregational life of the church before the watching world, he is there, and he is not silent.

Cessationists, standing in the tradition of B. B. Warfield, insist that the door to special revelation has been closed. Everything that mankind needs to know has been revealed. God has nothing more to say to his people. The book of Acts managed to squeak into the canon, but Luke wrote the last word, dotted the last *i*, crossed the last *t* and closed the book. With the passing of the last apostle everything Luke recorded in Acts became a moot point. The power of the Spirit at work in the world and the church, anything that was miraculous or supernatural, ceased. If you see it in the Bible but don't see it in the church today, don't be concerned, God has withdrawn that. It has ceased.

The contribution Pentecostals make to the discipline of hermeneutics is their insistence that God, by the Holy Spirit, continues to reveal himself to his people and the watching world. The cessationist is mistaken. The Bible is not a bound copy of propositions. The Spirit is more than a well polished idea archived in the proposition repository that we extract whenever we need to demonstrate our theological prowess. While affirming the transcendence of God, the otherness of God, we Pentecostals also affirm the immanence of God. Unlike the cessationist, who insists on transcendence to the detriment of immanence, Pentecostals bear witness to the preternatural activity of the Holy Spirit. This activity is called *experience*. Those who don't understand or those who oppose the Pentecostal witness of the immanence of the Spirit by the manifestation of his gifts appeal to the old saw that Pentecostals are hung up on tongues and other forms of experience. Usually they insist that experience must be measured by the written Word. Certainly this is true. Yet their declaration of the cessation of the gifts of the Spirit and the miraculous leaves little room for continuing dialogue. The intractable attitude of the cessationist toward the notion of the cessation of the charismata is as offensive to the Pentecostal as the Pentecostal's attitude toward the issue of tongues as the indicator of Spirit-baptism is offensive to the cessationist.

General revelation is a given. The physical reality that surrounds us is necessary and continues to reveal God to mankind. Special revelation takes us beyond physical reality into the realm of the Spirit. God reveals that part of himself that is transcendent and unknowable unless disclosed to us by the Holy Spirit. Cessationists contend that the transcendent knowing of God does not occur any longer. That means that all of the revelatory gifts of the Spirit set forth in 1 Corinthians 12 are no longer valid. If that is true it creates a serious hermeneutical problem, especially for Pentecostals and Charismatics. This is where Pentecostals, Charismatics, and traditionalists diverge.

Pentecostals and Charismatics do not accept the notion that any part of special revelation has ceased, particularly God's continuing disclosure of his person, his purpose, and his plan. Special revelation has not ceased. God still speaks. He continues to reveal himself by the Spirit's illumination of the written word. He still manifests himself through the exercise of the gifts of the Holy Spirit, continuing actions of the Spirit that reveal the power of God at work in the church and the world, now.

The reason Pentecostal scholars call for a hermeneutic that is particularly Pentecostal is that the present evangelical model makes no place for divine disclosure by way of the revelatory gifts mentioned by Paul in 1 Corinthians 12. When cessationists insist that the Holy Spirit has ceased to reveal the transcendent God, they have effectively created a God who does not speak or act.

When God no longer speaks, when he ceases to reveal himself through revelatory activity, God has been turned into a dumb idol and the Bible has become an iconic witness to itself instead of pointing beyond itself to the transcendent living, acting, speaking God of the New Testament. This must not be done. However, that is exactly what is done when the witness of believers whose experience of the charismata of the Spirit is devalued and denigrated. If God is only transcendent, as the cessationist argues, he is placed beyond the scope of human experience, and all we are left with is a book without substance. In essence we have a God who does not speak and a Bible that points only to itself.

There is a way out of this conundrum. It is called the incarnation. It was an idea conceived in the mind of God and consummated before a watching world on the day of Pentecost. There the transcendent God made a way to unravel the communication problem. It is an idea called immanence. Immanence is presence. What mankind needs is a God who is there, present, active, and not silent. On that first Christian Pentecost the promise of the Father was poured out, without measure, and he who is called Emmanuel was, at last, truly with us. By the gift of the person of the Holy Spirit the problem of the unreachable, transcendent God was resolved, once and for all. The presence of the Spirit active in the church provides the immanence we need to bring God near. It is this proximity of the Spirit and his activity that we call *experience*. It can also be called *revelation*, for what is experienced when people are baptized with the Spirit is an act of revelation on the part of God. Whenever a gift of healing is dispensed by the Spirit we are experiencing the immanence of God, who has come to us as the compassionate Savior.

Hermeneutically speaking, the question becomes, What do we do with scripture and experience that falls outside of the accepted special revelation parameters? If the Holy Spirit speaks or acts in the realm of extra-revelation, if he gives a word of knowledge, for example, what do we do with that activity? The traditionalist dispatches it quite handily: God doesn't do that anymore. The Pentecostal's response: God continues to speak and act in our midst; he still reveals himself to mankind. God is with us! Emmanuel!

TOWARD AN ADEQUATE HERMENEUTICAL MODEL

Pentecostal tradition exemplifies a hermeneutical principal that bears a sense of extra-revelation. We believe that God discloses himself to us, in a particular way, through the written word. The idea is that a person cannot simply pick up the Bible, read, and thereby perceive what God is saying; "the natural man does not understand the things of God" (1 Cor 2:14). Rather, we believe that God, through the Spirit, grants us a transcendent understanding of the word that we could not have with the natural mind. Since this is held to be true, some Pentecostals deem it unnecessary to receive formal training in order to properly interpret the word of God. The Holy Spirit will reveal to the seeker what a particular passage means. After all, the Spirit inspired the word to start with, why should he not reveal what it means now?

Karl Barth posits a theology of the word that is very similar, *in the sense that the Spirit illumines the word*, and though some have leveled the charge that Barth claims that the Scriptures merely *contain* the word of God and are *not* the word of God, as Bernard Ramm points out, this is a misunderstanding of Barth. For Barth, one must *seek* to understand what God is saying in Scripture. A person cannot use a mere rational approach to Scripture and hope to properly interpret its meaning. Ramm cites Barth's concept "that the Word of God is not immediately obvious in any of its chapters or verses. On the contrary, the truth of the Word must be *sought*" (his italics).[12] The reason for this is that there exists a *diastasis* (interval) between the original revelation of the word of God and our human comprehension and recording of that word. Ramm grants us insight into the idea of diastasis as used by Barth:

> The primal meaning of the Word of God is God in his self-disclosure; God in his act of revelation, which is (as it originates in God) infallible, inerrant, and indefectible. However, when the Word of God comes into the human sphere it undergoes a diffraction.
>
> The Word of God comes to the prophet or apostle in his language. No human language is a perfect mirror in which the Word of God is perfectly reflected. Hence a *diastasis* occurs at the point of language. The Word of God comes to the prophet, who is also a person existing in a given culture; hence the Word of God is stated in the terms and concepts of the prophet's culture. This translation creates a diastasis between the original Word of God and the

12. Ramm, *Fundamentalism*, 92.

cultural expression in Holy Scripture. The Word of God comes to the prophet and apostles, who, like all other people, are sinful. The sinful human mind does not reflect the pure Word of God, hence another diastasis emerges at this point.[13]

For Barth this diastasis, or interval, between the original revelation of God through the word of God and human reception and preservation of that word in written form must be bridged. This is accomplished through exegesis, meditation, and prayer. In other words, he appeals to the Spirit to operate through these practices to reveal to the seeker the meaning of Scripture so that it might indeed be *a living word of God* in our hearts. This model is not unlike the prevailing model in evangelical circles: exegesis, synthesis, and application. The emphasis upon the illuminating activity of the Spirit, however, would be understood somewhat differently. The prevailing evangelical model places the onus of interpretation upon the rational powers of the human mind as it labors to comprehend the meaning of Scripture. Barth's model places the impetus upon the work of the Spirit in the sense of there being *extra-revelation* granted to the interpreter that is *transcendent* in nature and wholly apart from the rational powers of the human mind. Not that those powers are not employed in the interpretive process, but that the understanding of the meaning of Scripture comes from the transcendent source of the Holy Spirit, whose presence (immanence) and activity reach across the diastasis and illuminate the word.

This concept is not at all inconsistent with Pentecostal thought. The Pentecostal has, almost from the beginning of the movement, expressed a dependence on the Spirit for *revelation*; revelation not in the sense of general or special revelation, but rather, in the sense of *extra-revelation*. Not extra-revelation with the import of being *beyond* existing general and special revelation, but as the notion of granting true comprehension of existing general and, particularly, special revelation. This is not be to understood as a gnostic idea, although, admittedly, there have been and are those who attach such a meaning to the concept. A gnostic notion in this regard is the exception and certainly not representative. *Extra-revelation*, in this instance, means that work of the Spirit that informs the human mind with an understanding of the meaning of the written word, whereby the *diastasis* existing in the translation of meaning from the original

13. Ibid., 90–91.

word of God into our human terminology through the various linguistic, cultural, and anthropocentric filters is bridged by the transcendent illumination of the Holy Spirit. Donald Bloesch, an esteemed scholar in the Evangelical and Reformed tradition, posits a view similar to Barth's:

> If the infallibility of the Bible were self-evident, if the divine truth of Scripture were directly accessible, then the hermeneutical task would be quite easy, but for better or worse it is much more complicated.
>
> We must first recognize that the Bible is not principally a source book of data on Israel's history (as Wellhausen alleges) but a witness to divine revelation, a witness that points beyond itself to a supernatural reality. This means that in order for us to come to a true understanding of the basic content of the Bible, our inward eyes must be opened to the divine message to which the texts attest. But this is no longer a matter of historical analysis and research but of spiritual discernment. The divine truth of the Bible can only be known by a miracle of divine grace.[14]

Bloesch would also advocate exegetical study, reflection, and prayer.

In like manner, Clark Pinnock offers a view that approximates that of Barth and Bloesch:

> My hermeneutical proposal is that we hear the Word of God in the interaction between the Word and the Spirit, not through Scripture alone and not by means of meditation alone. This makes interpretation an art rather than a science or technique. It is a skill that has to be acquired by a combination of study and prayer. It cannot be reduced to a set of rules.[15]

Pinnock explains how this idea of hermeneutics functions:

> There are two sides to hermeneutics. First, we listen to the text as God's Word in human language given to us, and second, we open ourselves to God's Spirit to reveal the particular significance the text has for the present situation. Interpretation involves a bipolar ellipse, and moves back and forth between the historical meaning of the Bible and our standing before God. It therefore involves fidelity to the text and creativity in the context. The first provides the objective content and control, the second opens us up to God's leading and direction. Thus, the interpreter is not autonomous

---

14. Bloesch, *Essentials,* 1:70–71.

15. Pinnock, *Scripture Principle,* 198.

but subject to the text, and avoids frozen legalism by being open
to God's Spirit. In this way errors of the left and the right can be
avoided.[16]

Though Pentecostals would not express this concept in exactly the
above manner, nevertheless, what Barth has posited and Bloesch and
Pinnock affirm, we, in principle endorse: In order to properly understand
the word of God we need the transcendent illumination of the Holy Spirit.
And we are exact and correct in that respect.[17]

It is this diastasis that prompts proper hermeneutical principles.
Hermeneutics involves that necessary *bridge building* we must do to
traverse the diastasis that exists between the word of God and our understanding of its meaning. Pentecostals, as all other believers, must begin the hermeneutical task by employing principles that the church has
formulated through the centuries. It is not for us to create a wholly new
hermeneutic in order to comprehend the meaning of Scripture. There is a
dimension we Pentecostals add to extant hermeneutics, but we must build
upon the existing hermeneutical foundation if we are to remain true to an
evangelical approach to Scripture, which we must surely do.

What we Pentecostals have to offer to the discipline of hermeneutics
has been identified for us by Barth, et al. It is the transcendent work of
the Holy Spirit in revealing to us the meaning of Scripture that would
otherwise be hidden from us by that diastasis that truly does exist. No
thinking Pentecostal should have trouble with that. We do not rely on our
cleverness or our education to illumine God's word; rather, we acknowledge our dependence upon the Spirit to accomplish that necessity. This is
correct and proper.

However, there is something lacking, for the most part, in Pentecostal
hermeneutical labors. Note that Barth insists that a proper hermeneutical
model is threefold. First, sound hermeneutics requires exegesis, something
at which we Pentecostals have certainly been remiss. The failure to properly exegete a passage of Scripture has often lead to a misinterpretation
of the passage. The Spirit of God uses our intelligence, not our ignorance.
Thanks to Hebrew and Greek scholars, there are ample exegetical tools
available in book stores, the use of which will enable one to do exegesis
adequately. No one should think they cannot do proper exegesis. You may

16. Ibid., 197–98.
17. See also Morris, *Revelation*, 92–108.

not do it as well as a professional would, but it can be done. Good exegesis takes time. It is not for the lazy or the impatient. However, it is the correct place for the Christian leader to start if there is to be a competent interpretation of Scripture, if we are to reach across the chasm of the diastasis and grasp the true meaning of God's word for our day.

It is interesting that the last thing Barth said to his fellow believers before he escaped Nazi Germany was, "Exegesis, exegesis, and yet more exegesis! Keep to the Word, to the scripture that has been given us."[18] He knew that if the confessing church in Germany was to remain true to her Lord she would need the solid foundation of correctly interpreted Scripture. That is also true of the Pentecostal movement. We have already witnessed the devastation wreaked upon our movement by people claiming to have received extra-revelation from the Spirit that was absolutely contrary to a proper understanding of the word and ways of God; in particular, the *Jesus Only* movement and the *Latter Rain* movement, both of which rose out of the Pentecostal movement, due to too much subjectivity in the hermeneutical task. The combination of exegesis, theological reflection, and prayer would have certainly reduced the probability of these two aberrations coming into existence.

The second aspect of hermeneutics Barth insists on is meditation. This is often referred to as theological reflection. Both meditation and theological reflection refer to the same thing: waiting upon the Spirit, making available to him all of our faculties, the results of our exegetical studies, and our listening spirit. It is here, in this reflective mode, that the Spirit will illuminate the word to our hearts and cause us to understand what God is saying to his church and his world.

Third, Barth enjoins us to prayer. This is something that Pentecostals surely know how to do. We have been people of prayer from the beginning of our movement. However, our praying can certainly be more focused and effective if we come to it with the holistic sense that it is part and parcel of the threefold hermeneutical process.

It would be a misconception to think we must separate exegesis from theological reflection and theological reflection from prayer and prayer from both of them. Each part of this hermeneutical model should become an integrated whole. We are to pray while we do exegesis. We are to reflect while we pray and do exegesis. We are to do exegesis while we

---

18. Fee, *Exegesis*, dedication page.

reflect and pray. It is the involvement of the believer in the hermeneutical model, in its entirety, that makes available to the Spirit one who can be illumined with the truth of the word. That is competent hermeneutical practice. What a powerful combination that can be!

Extra-revelation in any form must be bound by these interpretive guidelines. Extra-revelation must always be subject to a competent understanding of the written word. It must never stand contrary to the written word that has been properly interpreted through the use of exegesis, theological reflection, and prayer. The safeguard of subjecting extra-revelation to competent exegetical and hermeneutical oversight will serve to protect our movement from the aberrations we have experienced in our history. Perhaps this is the concern that lies behind McLean's appeal for a Pentecostal hermeneutic. If we as a movement, and its various denominations in particular, do not embrace a more competent hermeneutical model, such as the threefold model above, we shall be doomed to become, as McLean has expressed, *religious oddities.*

The need is not that we Pentecostals should develop a hermeneutic which is *distinct* in order to preserve theological concepts that we deem to be distinct; rather, the need is that we Pentecostals begin to practice hermeneutics in a competent manner, utilizing all of the hermeneutical tools available to us. Tools that have been around for a long time but have been rejected as unspiritual or ignored. Tools that can lead us to a more mature understanding of the faith and to an adjustment in our theology when it does not stand the test of competent hermeneutical practice.

AN EPISTEMOLOGICAL PERSPECTIVE

Phillip Wiebe, an Evangelical scholar, discusses the hermeneutics of the initial evidence doctrine from an epistemological perspective. The idea of evidence, according to Wiebe, is an epistemological one. "This means that it has to do with situations in which one event is taken as providing grounds for believing that another event has occurred." Evidential claims can be of different sorts, confirming or undermining, or they could be irrelevant. Evidence can be conclusive, either in affirming or in denying a matter. Evidential claims must be understood as being different from causal claims, while there may be a correlation between them. Wiebe points out that evidence in and of itself connotes a sense of time-independence, whereas the introduction of the idea of *initial* "introduces a temporal element, for it suggests that there is such a thing as *first evidence*." First evidence, contends Wiebe, can be understood in two ways: (1) "It is evidence that happens to be the first that is encountered in the investigation of a reasonable hypothesis, or," (2) "that it is evidence that happens to be the first that an investigator considers when assessing the reasonableness of a hypothesis."[19] Wiebe asks, and rightly so, which is it that Pentecostals mean in speaking of initial evidence? Do we mean that glossolalia is the first evidence that always happens or that it is the first that one considers when investigating claims of Spirit-baptism? Most Pentecostals would probably opt for the first of these choices and include the possibility of the second. Wiebe contends that this turns out to be a peculiar claim. With the addition of the word *initial* to the formula it is implied that there are various evidences that would be as valid but that glossolalia just happens to be the first of these to become evident.[20]

Wiebe insists that this becomes a strange claim:

> The initial evidence doctrine would then be a universal claim about what evidence people happen to find or look for when attempting to establish whether someone is baptized in the Spirit—that is, the initial evidence doctrine would be reduced to a universal claim about the epistemological activities of those interested in determining whether someone is baptized in the Spirit. It would not be a theological or doctrinal claim at all. I do not think that this is what pentecostalists holding to the initial evidence doctrine have wanted to claim.[21]

He posits that what Pentecostals may actually mean is the conjunction of two theses: glossolalia is evidence of Spirit-baptism and glossolalia is the first physical effect of Spirit-baptism. The second of these, Wiebe maintains, infers a causal relationship between the two and not just an evidential one. That is, glossolalia is caused by the baptism with the Spirit, and since it is considered to be *a first effect* this initial effect implies a temporal sequence, first, second, etc.

Wiebe then applies this understanding to the initial evidence doctrine relative to its meaning. It can have these six meanings:

1. Glossolalia is evidence that one has been baptized in the Spirit.

19. Wiebe, "Initial Evidence," 467–68.
20. Ibid., 465.
21. Ibid., 468.

2. Glossolalia is the only evidence that one has been baptized in the Spirit.

3. Glossolalia is a causal effect of one's being baptized in the Spirit.

4. Glossolalia is the first effect of Spirit baptism.

5. The capacity for glossolalia is an effect of Spirit baptism.

6. The capacity for glossolalia is evidence of one's having been baptized in the Spirit.

These variants were determined by Wiebe from an exegetical analysis of Acts and its pertinent passages. Of these possible meanings most Pentecostals would affirm only 1, 3, or 4. However, I have come across some Pentecostals in my sixty-plus year sojourn in the Pentecostal movement who would endorse 2.

Wiebe offers these conclusions relative to the above stated variants:

> It seems to me that the most that defenders of pentecostal views can claim concerning the relationship between glossolalia and Spirit baptism is that glossolalia is evidence (but not conclusive evidence) that Spirit baptism has occurred and that glossolalia, when it does occur, is probably caused by Spirit baptism. The view that glossolalia is the first effect of Spirit baptism receives no conclusive textual support. If that is what the initial evidence doctrine is taken to mean or at least imply, it is unfortunately indefensible.[22]

I do not think we Pentecostals intend to convey the idea that glossolalia is, indeed, the first effect of Spirit-baptism. We would affirm that there are internal effects occurring during Spirit-baptism that are not verifiable in this sense and that they take place prior to any outward manifestation of the Spirit. What seems to be intended is that glossolalia should be viewed as the first verifiable evidence occurring *at the time* one is experiencing Spirit-baptism. Certainly, we cannot determine what is happening in the human spirit when it is being inundated by the Holy Spirit. Anything that could be said in that regard would be pure speculation. However, typically, Pentecostals would affirm that glossolalic utterance is to be viewed as the first verifiable evidence, at the time of Spirit-baptism, that a person has been Spirit-filled. Understood in this manner, an initial evidence doctrine could be palatable for many Christians.

22. Ibid., 469–71.

The language employed in formulating the initial evidence construct indicates that other evidences would be expected to denote that one had been Spirit-baptized. Were this idea to be carried to its logical conclusion it would demand that these other evidences must exist in order to confirm the validity of a person's Spirit-baptism.

R. Hollis Gause, a Pentecostal scholar (CGCT), devotes a chapter in his book *Living in the Spirit,* titled "The Moral and Spiritual Evidences of the Baptism of the Holy Spirit," to this concern. He contends that in Spirit-baptism "the Holy Spirit accomplishes in those to whom He ministers the grace of His own nature. In terms of law He accomplishes that which is required, which is the holiness of His own nature. In terms of promise, He accomplishes graces of love and mercy therein promised, which is the formation of His nature in us."[23]

Gause continues with this observation:

> We conclude, then, that the preaching of the kingdom of God makes certain ethical demands. . . . It is impossible to claim participation in the Kingdom which is formed by the presence and ministry of the Holy Spirit without also accepting the dictation of His holiness, truth, and love. This Holy Spirit is the Spirit of grace and the implanter of grace in men. He is the Spirit of all the graces which belong to the nature of Christ. Their presence is witness of His presence. The prime evidence of a Holy Spirit-filled life is the visibility of Christ in the believer. It is the work of the baptism of the Holy Spirit to cultivate these evidences.[24]

A SUMMARY

First, we must consider the question of the need for a particular Pentecostal hermeneutic. Here I believe it has been determined that there is not a need for a hermeneutic that is especially Pentecostal. Rather, we Pentecostals need to embrace an existing hermeneutical model, one that stands solidly in the evangelical tradition and one that complements our prevailing attitude toward Scripture; that is, one that readily acknowledges that it is the Spirit of God who truly illumines the word and grants us understanding of its truth.

23. Gause, *Living,* 472.
24. Ibid., 96.

This is the concept of *extra-revelation*, that is, the affirmation that there is special revelation that is not considered by the traditionalist to be continuing revelatory acts of God. The gifts of the Holy Spirit named by Paul in 1 Corinthians 12 are the word of wisdom, the word of knowledge, faith, healing, miracles, prophecy, discernment of spirits, speaking in tongues, and interpretation. The term extra-revelation is used to distinguish these gifts excluded by the traditionalist. This is the Pentecostal's contribution to extant hermeneutics. Our task, then, is to welcome a hermeneutical model, such as Barth's, and employ that model's principles in working through hermeneutical endeavors competently. Employing such a model will give Pentecostals, both scholars and others, the opportunity to render interpretation of Scripture in a more precise manner, helping us to steer clear of hermeneutical foibles such as those our movement has encountered in the past. The model also provides us with the medium by which we can subject every form of extra-revelation to the scrutiny of the word of God, thereby providing us with the much needed preventative device to serve as the walls McLean speaks of that keep us exuberant souls from falling over the edge.[25] Also, it will grant us the ability to properly interpret the word in the ongoing theological labors we now struggle with as we attempt to refine, define, and redefine our theology.

It is my conviction that the model offered by Barth is one that Pentecostals should look to in a serious manner for the development of hermeneutical procedure. The model challenges us to stand in the Evangelical tradition and approach the Scriptures both objectively and subjectively. Objectively, we are to do the necessary exegesis in order to understand the text, not only in its written context but its historical/cultural context as well. This objective work would include the philological aspects—consideration of literary genre and grammatical concerns. Subjectively, our task would include theological reflection, prayer, and finally *hearing* the word the Lord desires us to hear as the Spirit grants illumination. Exegesis, meditation, and prayer, is a strong three-fold integrated methodology in seeking a competent understanding of the word of God. Such a model will afford the checks and balances sorely needed by our movement, loaded as it is with a propensity for the spontaneous, in order to preserve our faith in its Evangelical/Pentecostal heritage.

25. McLean, "Hermeneutic," 49.

Equipped with the tools of a sound hermeneutical model, Pentecostals should move from an apologetic approach to theology to a stance that is aggressive and affirmative. We need to move from a posture of defending our faith to one of proclaiming our faith; that is, explaining it in a precise and articulate way. We should not approach these matters with an obscurantist mentality but must forthrightly grapple with the tough issues we face as we labor to understand our movement and explain it to the larger church and the watching world. We should acknowledge that we have approached the book of Acts as though it was written to be a didactic instrument and have exacted from it conclusions that do not bear the stress of sound hermeneutical procedures.

Consideration should be given to the challenge laid down by Wiebe. Perhaps the problem is semantic and we need to reword our evidential statements. As we have already posited, surely we Pentecostals would not want to say that glossolalia is the *first effect* of Spirit-baptism. We must acknowledge that the indwelling Spirit is present prior to this filling experience and that He is at work in one's interior in a manner unobservable to others. This demands that we concur that this baptismal work, whatever it may be, is accomplished by the Spirit in the human spirit and is indeed the first effect of that baptism. This would mean that any glossolalic manifestation could, at best, be labeled the first *verifiable* evidence available to observers at the time of a person's Spirit-baptism. It may well be that Wiebe is then correct in insisting that such an evidential statement would be more epistemological than theological or doctrinal.

If one could endorse the above consideration, it appears that it would be necessary to make an adjustment in our insistence that glossolalia is the *primary* evidence that a person has been Spirit-filled. There is a vast difference between affirming that glossolalia is the first *verifiable* evidence and stating that it is the *primary* evidence.

The first idea (that glossolalia is the first *verifiable* evidence) indicates that tongues-speech may be expected and that when it does appear it may serve as a verifying indicator that the person is experiencing Spirit-baptism. It acknowledges the fact that we, as observers, cannot actually perceive what the Spirit is doing in the human spirit yet recognizes that he is there already giving life to that spirit and working to bring it into the fullness of Jesus Christ. The second idea (that glossolalia is the *primary* evidence) demands that one speak with tongues, the absence of which indicates that the person has not experienced Spirit-baptism. This notion limits the evidential concerns to evidence that is only verifiable by observers, ignoring the internal ministry of the Spirit in the believer. Though a believer may have been ministered to powerfully by the Spirit's baptism, if observers do not *see* some external demonstration of that ministry, it is concluded, by the observers, that the person was not Spirit-baptized.

By not limiting the evidence to a charismatic indicator but also expecting that there will be ethical indicators, the first construct leaves the door open for further verification of Spirit-baptism. The terminology *initial* has already opened that possibility in the present construct. *Initial* implies that there will be other evidences. This goes hand in glove with early considerations of Spirit-baptism, when our forefathers affirmed the purpose of this baptism as being the believer's equipment with power for holy living and effective service. *Holy living* is the ethical dimension of the Christian life, while the matter of *service* touches upon the charismatic dimension of that life.

As we have seen in Gause's comments, the indwelling Spirit brings with him his holy character as well as his gifts of grace. His very presence in the believer causes that person to be both holy and charismatic, for both of these are part of the Spirit's nature and of his ministry of imparting God's *charis* (grace) to God's people.

Both the ethical and the charismatic aspects of the Christian life are of great importance, but a perusal of Scripture will inform us that the scales are weighted on the side of the ethical evidences. In both 1 Corinthians 12 and Galatians 5, Paul insists that the ethical evidence is primary. "Though I speak with the tongues of men and of angels but have not love . . ." It is of great significance that the great outpouring of God's Spirit in this twentieth century was granted to, of the many Christian bodies available, a people whose primary concern was with the ethical issues of life—the Holiness movement! That fact should speak volumes to us!

What we have said here is in no manner to be considered a denigration of the value and the importance of the charismatic dimension. It is indispensable, but God considers the ethical dimension to be of greater importance. "And now I will show you the most excellent way" (1 Cor 12:31). Here Paul leads his readers from concerns with charismata to matters pertaining to the ethical dimension of life. Following 12:31 is one of mankind's most profound ethical statements ever penned, 1 Corinthians 13.

The second construct (that glossolalia is the primary evidence of Spirit-baptism) does not insist upon the ethical dimension as evidential.

Only the charismatic dimension is of primary interest. As we have seen in our study thus far, this poses a very dangerous situation for our movement, for it allows for anyone who may exhibit glossolalia to insist that they have been Spirit-baptized, even though that person's relationships with other believers and the world at large may not buttress that claim.

I do not advocate a return to the misconstrued legalistic notions that many have had in the past as to what constitutes holiness. However, I do call for an evidential construct that provides for evidences that can be produced in the believer's life by the Holy Spirit and *only* by the Holy Spirit. Evidences that address the ethical concerns so paramount in the word of God that they must not be ignored. Evidences that not only express the charismatic dimension of the Spirit but demonstrate his ethical nature as well.

All of this is involved in the hermeneutical challenge we face as Pentecostals. Only an adequate hermeneutical model and sound practice can help us resolve these considerations.

8

Tongues as the Normative Evidence

THE THEOLOGICAL IDEA WE will now consider was first developed by a group of Bible school students at Charles Fox Parham's Bethel Bible school in Topeka, Kansas, in the closing days of the first year of the twentieth century.[1]

This doctrine, known as the *initial evidence doctrine*, originated in the U.S. about one hundred years ago. As was observed in the introduction of this work, T. B. Barratt and George Jeffreys, prominent European Pentecostal leaders, did not subscribe to the initial evidence concept. Walter Hollenweger makes this very point:

> Both inside and outside pentecostalism there is criticism of this doctrine and practice. Important Pentecostal churches (for example, in Chile or certain countries in Europe) disagree with the doctrine of "the initial physical sign" and believe that the baptism of the Holy Spirit is not always accompanied by this sign. In fact in many Pentecostal churches a great proportion of the members (and sometimes even some of the pastors) have never spoken in tongues. How the Assemblies of God and other similar bodies are going to solve this conflict between their doctrine and their praxis is an open question.[2]

There is an accepted myth, at least in the Assemblies of God, that the initial evidence doctrine has always been an uncontested doctrinal concept. Such is not the case. It is difficult to discern the substance of the

---

1. It must be noted that though I use Parham's Bible school as the starting point in this discussion, the original Pentecostal outpouring in America occurred among a group of holiness people at a meeting in Camp Creek, Cherokee County, North Carolina, led by W. F. Bryant, a layman, in 1896. This group eventually became what is now known as the Church of God (Cleveland, TN). See Conn, *Mighty Army*, 24–27.

2. Hollenweger, "Twenty Years' Research," 7.

debates regarding the formulation of this doctrine in the Assemblies of God between 1912 and 1918; however, a perusal of archived material indicates that all was not smiles and the right hand of fellowship. The General Council of 1917 passed a resolution requiring credentialed ministers to endorse the Fundamental Truths adopted at the Council of 1916.[3] Until the Council of 1916 there was no consensus on doctrine. In the statement of faith adopted at the General Council of 1916, article 6 reads as follows: "The full consummation of the baptism of believers in the Holy Ghost and fire, is indicated by the initial sign of speaking in tongues, as the Spirit of God gives utterance. Acts 2:4. This wonderful experience is distinct from and subsequent to the experience of the new birth. Acts 10:44–46; 11:14–16; 15:8, 9."[4]

Fred Francis Bosworth joined the Pentecostal movement at Zion, Illinois, in 1906 and was one of the participants in the founding council of the Assemblies of God at Hot Springs, Arkansas, in April 1914.[5] Bosworth became very vocal in opposing the initial evidence doctrine when it became evident that those who were pushing its acceptance were winning the day. This would seem to indicate that there were a number of ministers who had questions about article 6 of the Fundamentals, and Bosworth may have been acting as their spokesman. Bosworth's opinion had apparently influenced a sufficient number of other ministers (or they simply held the same opinion themselves) that the General Council of 1918 found it necessary to debate the issue and adopt a resolution affirming the doctrine. It also appears that there was no open forum for a continuing debate on the matter until the Council of 1918.

Perusal of the Assembles of God literature of that day (*The Weekly Evangel* and the *Christian Evangel*, forerunners of the *Pentecostal Evangel*) reveals that the only position aired was pro-initial evidence. Evidently, those who controlled the fledgling fellowship's printed media determined which doctrinal position would hold sway by suppressing dissemination of the dissenting opinion.

---

3. As a result of this action, approximately twenty-six percent of the credentialed ministers (more than 150 of 585) of the Assemblies of God were dropped from the roles. This involved more than the initial evidence doctrine, however, and included "The New Issue" (Jesus Only), the oneness doctrine that resulted in the unitarian Pentecostals. See Blumhofer, "Debate."

4. General Council of the Assemblies of God, "Minutes," 11.

5. Blumhofer, *Assemblies of God*, 52; see also Menzies, *Anointed*, 319–20.

On July 24, 1918, under considerable pressure and for conscience' sake, Bosworth submitted his resignation from the infant denomination to General Chairman J. W. Welch.[6] By the time of the 1918 Council, therefore, the strong voice opposing the doctrine had already been effectively silenced. Bosworth affiliated with the Christian and Missionary Alliance when he withdrew from the Assemblies of God. He wrote a book on the ministry of divine healing, *Christ the Healer*, republished in 1973 by Fleming H. Revell Company.

It is apparent, based on this information, that the American *initial evidence doctrine* had opposition from within the movement at its very inception and does not enjoy a history of consensus, as is popularly thought.

AN OLD IDEA—A NEW MEANING

The term "baptism of the Holy Spirit" was not coined by Parham or his followers. The popular use of the term found its roots in the Holiness movement, of which both Parham and those who followed him were an integral part, and it predominantly held the meaning of that act of the Spirit called the second work of grace, sanctification. Donald Dayton documents this in his work on the development of the doctrine of Spirit-baptism, demonstrating that around the time of the Civil War there began to emerge the use of *pentecostal* terms and concepts in the Holiness movement.[7]

Allen Clayton rightly observes: "It was this pneumatocentrism, founded upon the book of Acts, emphasizing the eventness of the holiness experience, and seeking for an unimpeachable sign of assurance that Spirit baptism had taken place, which led to the birth of the pentecostal movement."[8]

R. A. Torrey was probably the person most influential in calling attention to the person and work of the Holy Spirit in the closing days of the nineteenth century. His book *How to Obtain Fullness of Power*, published in 1897, devotes an extensive chapter to the ministry of the Spirit. Other titles written by Torrey in that era were *The Person & Work of the Holy Spirit* (1910), and *The Baptism of the Holy Spirit* (n.d.)

---

6. Bosworth to Welch, 1918, Assemblies of God Archives.

7. Dayton, "Doctrine," 114–26.

8. Clayton, "William H. Durham," 37.

A book by John MacNeil, *The Spirit Filled Life*, was published in 1896. Andrew Murray, who wrote the introduction to MacNeil's book, produced a work entitled *Full Blessing of Pentecost*. All of these works dealt with what was termed "the Baptism with the Holy Spirit." Though the topic was handled somewhat differently from the way a twentieth-century Pentecostal would approach the subject, nevertheless, these and similar writings of this period exerted profound influence upon the soon to emerge Pentecostal movement.

When Parham assigned the students of his Bible school the task of determining a biblical evidence of the fullness of the Spirit he was reflecting directly upon the current usage of the term, that is, that Spirit-baptism was the sanctification of the believer. Various preachers and teachers were claiming different evidences to bear witness that a person had experienced this work of the Spirit. The concern with an evidence indicating that one had, indeed, received the fullness or baptism with the Spirit was not that others might become convinced—and this very important—it was that the person *receiving* might have the assurance of Spirit-baptism.[9] In our day, the emphasis on an evidence has shifted from assurance for the believer to being a sign convincing others that one has experienced the fullness of the Spirit. A very popular question asked in Pentecostal and Charismatic circles is, "Do you speak in tongues?" The implication is that if one can affirm that one does, the questioner will know that the questioned has, indeed, received the fullness of the Spirit.

Nonetheless, Parham's motivation in assigning this task to his students was to find a biblical evidence to use as a plum line for distinguishing between what was genuine and what was false in Spirit-baptism, that is, the second work of grace, sanctification.[10] This concern for the genuine activity of the Spirit is seen later in Parham's dealing with the fleshly aberrations at the Azusa Street Mission in Los Angeles.

Lilian Thistlethwaite, sister of Parham's wife, Sarah, and one of the students, informs us that it was just prior to the Christmas holidays in 1900 that the students of Bethel took up the study of this work of the Holy Spirit. Before leaving for Kansas City for several speaking engagements Parham gave the students these instructions:

---

9. Lindsell, *Holy Spirit*, 121.

10. Parham, *Charles F. Parham*, 52.

Students, as I have studied the teachings in the various Bible Schools and full gospel movements, conviction, conversion, healing and sanctification are taught virtually the same, but on the baptism there is a difference among them. Some accept Steven Merrit's teaching of baptism at sanctification, while others say this is only the anointing and there is a baptism received through the "laying on of hands" or the gift of the Holy Ghost, yet they agree on no definite evidence. Some claim the fulfillment of promise "by faith" without any special witness, while others, because of the wonderful blessings or demonstrations, such as shouting or jumping. Though I honor the Holy Ghost in anointing power both in conversion and in sanctification, yet I believe there is a greater revelation of His power. The gifts are in the Holy Spirit and with the baptism of the Holy Spirit the gifts, as well as the graces, should be manifested. Now, students, while I am gone, see if there is not some evidence given of the baptism so there may be no doubt on the subject. We see the signs already being fulfilled that mark the soon coming of the Lord and I believe with John Wesley that at Christ's second coming the Church will be found with the same power that the Apostles and the early Church possessed.[11]

Following this charge to his students, Parham was absent for three days. Upon his return, having completed their study of the book of Acts, the student body presented him with the evidential notion that now holds sway in most Pentecostal circles. According to Thistlethwaite: "On Mr. Parham's return to the school with his friends, he asked the students whether they had found any Bible evidence of the baptism of the Holy Spirit. The answer was, unanimous, 'speaking in other tongues.'"[12]

IS THE NORMATIVE ARGUMENT HERMENEUTICALLY SOUND?

Our task here is to make a determination as to whether this evidential concept can stand the test of sound biblical, theological, and hermeneutical analysis.

The argument involved in the formulation of this concept has been termed the *normative* argument. What this essentially means is that the book of Acts offers an evidence that appears to be the normal pattern of the Holy Spirit when he baptizes people in his fullness. This is based upon

11. Parham, *Charles F. Parham*, 58–59.

12. Ibid., 59.

the pattern of the five instances of Spirit-baptism recorded in the book of Acts (2:1–42, 8:4–24, 9:1–10, 10:1–48, 19:1–7).[13]

Carl Brumback expresses the notion common to normative statements when he insists that Spirit-baptism in "its initial oncoming, . . . was signalized by utterances by the one hundred and twenty in languages never learned by them. It is our belief that the speaking in tongues on that occasion formed the pattern for *every* singular baptism or charismatic enduement."[14]

In a questionable interpretation of Acts 2:39, Thomas Holdcroft, a Canadian Pentecostal, argues:

> On Biblical grounds, tongues are a necessary and essential evidence of the baptism of the Spirit. Believers may enjoy various remarkable experiences with God and His Spirit, but if they do not speak in tongues, their experience *is not the baptism of the Holy Spirit*. God promised that the Biblical pattern *was the standard for future times*: "The promise is unto you, and to your children, and to all that are afar off" (Acts 2:39). What was true at the Day of Pentecost, and on subsequent occasions in Scripture, must continue to be true throughout the age.[15]

Holdcroft makes the unsupported assumption that *the promise* in Acts 2:39 is the pattern of glossolalic utterance Pentecostals have perceived in Luke's record. This pattern is considered to be *the standard for future times*. Holdcroft's contention is that Luke *intended* to convey to the church of his day and to future generations of Christians that glossolalia is the primary evidence of Spirit-baptism. Such an interpretation simply will not stand up under proper hermeneutical procedure. The promise Luke makes reference to in Acts 2:39 is the *person* of the Holy Spirit, not some *manifestation* of the Spirit. We must not confuse the charisms of the Spirit with the person of the Spirit. The church down through the centuries has had the Spirit at work within her, even in the most somber days of the Dark Ages. The Holy Spirit did not leap over the centuries from the upper room in Jerusalem to Camp Creek, North Carolina, or a Bible school in Topeka, Kansas, leaving everything in between in a vacuum. God did not start something different with Agnes Ozman. The church

13. See Walston, *Tongues Controversy,* 183–201.

14. Brumback, *What Meaneth This?* 198 (emphasis mine).

15. Holdcroft, *Holy Spirit,* 122–23.

has been living in the era of the Spirit from the first pentecostal outpouring on the day of Pentecost to this very day. It is true that his person and work were obscured by other interests and emphases. It was, indeed, necessary that he be brought from that obscurity into a balanced focus and emphasis in the twentieth century. The promise of the Father had to be affirmed and embraced by a new generation of believers. That is true of each succeeding generation. But at no time can we rightly say that the *given*, poured out Spirit was not active in the church. The church cannot exist without his presence. It simply would not be the church.

Are we Pentecostals willing to say of those persons who bore the testimony of God's redeeming grace from generation to generation, until it reached us who live in this century, that they did not possess the Holy Spirit? Yet most of those saints who lived between apostolic times and our day did not exercise tongues-speech. By what Spirit did they live? If they are part of the church they belong to Christ, and as the apostle has duly informed us, "if any man have not the Spirit of Christ, he does not belong to Christ" (Rom 8:9).

Myer Pearlman is correct when he insists that regeneration occurs by faith and repentance and that this regeneration, by the Spirit, involves a union between the Father and the Son with the believer, "which is known as indwelling."[16] Pearlman further insists, "It cannot be denied that there is a real sense in which all truly regenerated persons have the Spirit."[17]

Frank Lindblad, a Pentecostal pioneer in the Pacific Northwest, supports this idea:

> But someone says, "Has not the Holy Spirit been imparted to all believers? Then what need we more?" The Holy Spirit has been imparted to all believers for without Him no salvation could take place or exist. The very witness of salvation comes thru the Holy Spirit. The Spirit Himself beareth witness with our spirit, that we are children of God.[18]

Therefore, we cannot construe Acts 2:39 to mean that the promise of the Spirit to the church equals the charism of glossolalia. It simply is not the case. The promise is the Holy Spirit in all of his fullness and power, not just one gift or manifestation.

---

16. Pearlman, *Doctrines*, 307.

17. Ibid., 311.

18. Lindblad, *Spirit*, 90.

A HERMENEUTICAL ANALYSIS

Some questions must be posed: Can this genre of biblical literature be used to establish such a doctrine, and can it continue to lend support to the doctrine of tongues as *primary* evidence of Spirit-baptism? The book of Acts is essentially a historical narrative. Was it the intent of Luke, as he wrote the book of Acts, to intimate to us that this was the way believers *always* experienced Spirit-baptism? Did he intend to establish a *pattern*? Is his record of such events exhaustive? Can we establish doctrine or theology on the basis of what is discovered in literature that was written, not for didactic purposes, but for telling the story of the developing church?

Was the intent of Luke in writing Acts to establish doctrine? Sound hermeneutics demands that we make these determinations if we are going to retain theological ideas based upon this genre—historical reporting. Did Luke intend that his narrative should be considered exhaustive? Or could what was said of the acts of Jesus Christ recorded in the gospel of John be equally true of the Holy Spirit: "Jesus did many other things as well. If every one of them were written down, I suppose that even the whole world would not have room for the books that would be written" (John 21:25). Granted, John is using hyperbole, however, he makes the point that Jesus did many other significant things that John did not record in his gospel.

If Luke's record cannot be considered to be exhaustive, (an exhaustive record would be difficult to determine, and most Evangelical New Testament scholarship indicates that Luke was selective of material included in both his gospel and the Acts), then we must logically determine that there *may have been* instances when believers of that era of the Spirit received his fullness without the accompanying glossolalia. In fact, part of the historical record provided by Luke in Acts does appear to offer such incidents, even though we Pentecostals desire to redact glossolalia into those records. We must conclude that we simply do not have enough information to make dogmatic assertions one way or the other.

Roger Stronstad has proffered the thesis that since Luke may be considered to be a theologian as well as a historian, it is proper to use the Acts narrative for didactic purposes. However, the weakness in this argument is the arbitrary assumption that since Luke may have been of a theological bent that was particularly his own, one may also assume that his *intent* in Acts is didactic. That all men are theological is true, however, the precision of a person's theology will vary greatly relative to that person's intentional focus on theological concerns. It remains questionable that Luke's intent in Acts demonstrates an overt theological pattern. If such was his intent he is very subtle with his theology.[19]

How is it that Luke, who in his gospel and the book of Acts writes with cohesion and clarity, almost meticulous in his expression of what he is conveying, comes to that part of truth that would truly call for crystal clear communication and suddenly decides to play hide-and-seek with his readers? Are we actually supposed to believe that the Spirit of God, who is pledged to lead us into all truth, decides to play games with us regarding Luke's purpose in writing the book of Acts? Is Luke, a gentile physician, so crafty and subtle that he *buries* a paradigm in his historical record that infers, doctrinally, that the proof that people are Spirit-baptized is speaking in an unknown tongue? Why not simply state outright that is the case? Is there an indication that Luke has used this device of subtlety to communicate other doctrinal information that is not obvious?

A BASIC PENTECOSTAL ASSUMPTION

We Pentecostals make a significant basic assumption relative to glossolalia that affects our interpretation of the glossolalic events in Acts. The assumption is that glossolalia first appeared within the realm of human experience on the day of Pentecost. This is reflected in Brumback's statement:

> It seems logical to conclude that it was God's will that the new experience, *so distinctly a part of the new dispensation,* should be made manifest by a *new sign.* Hence at Pentecost the disciples spoke with other tongues, an *unprecedented* manifestation, which became the immediate, outward result of every complete baptism or filling with the Holy Spirit *from that time forth,* notwithstanding its absence in pre-Pentecostal experiences.[20]

G. Raymond Carlson, a former General Superintendent of the Assemblies of God, in a 1976 publication echoed Brumback's contention that the day of Pentecost was the first appearance of glossolalia in human history,

> In the Book of Acts speaking with tongues is the authenticating evidence of the baptism in the Holy Spirit, just as prophecy, wis-

19. See Stronstad, *Charismatic Theology,* 9–11.
20. Brumback, *What Meaneth This?* 274 (emphasis mine).

dom, discernment, healing, miracles, and casting out of demons were under the old covenant; but *never before had anyone spoken in tongues*...[21]

Henry Ness, a Pentecostal pioneer in the Pacific Northwest, makes a similar statement: "Speaking with tongues as the Holy Spirit gives the utterance is the *unique* spiritual gift identified with the Church of Jesus Christ (1 Corinthians 12 and 14)."[22]

However, as has been demonstrated from historical records, the foregoing assumption is in error. Glossolalia, far from being a new phenomenon, had been around hundreds of years prior to the Pentecost event. The fact that the glossolalic utterances appeared in the context of pagan religion does not allow for discounting the reality of the phenomenon. That it was either psychic or demonic in origin gives no reason to ignore the fact of its presence within human experience prior to the disciples' encounter with the Holy Spirit and their subsequent glossolalic expressions. The argument that this was a unique and unheard of phenomenon can only be made from ignorance of the facts.

An insistence on maintaining such a stance in the face of historical fact hardly makes us credible as purveyors of the truth. To ignore the fact of prior glossolalia or to try to explain it away will only cause Pentecostals to appear obscurantist in mentality, which in turn would lower our credibility with thinking people inside or outside of the church. Therefore, we must set aside this assumption as invalid and unworthy of serious consideration. Also, in setting it aside we must come to terms with the fact that our affirming this assumption has colored our hermeneutics regarding the place of glossolalia in the event of Spirit-baptism. The idea of the uniqueness of tongues has led to the notion that it is the primary evidence in Spirit-baptism.

It is also true that we must disabuse ourselves of the notion that Luke wrote the book of Acts in the manner in which he did with the express intent of conveying to future generations of Christians that the early church considered glossolalia to be the primary sign that one has received the fullness of the Spirit.

A perusal of church history will set the record straight in this regard. Pentecostal historian Stanley Burgess informs us that "among those doc-

21. Carlson, *Spiritual Dynamics*, 67 (emphasis mine).
22. Ness, *Dunamis*, 49.

trines which remained largely undeveloped in the pre-Nicene period was that of the Holy Spirit."[23] As William Rusch points out, there was not a full blown theology of the Spirit present in the early church. There was not even a consensus regarding the person and work of the Spirit. Tertullian (d.c. 220) is the first Father prior to the fourth century to present a theology of the Spirit in a clear and precise manner.[24]

There was a considerable divergence of views about the Holy Spirit in the early history of the church. While it is accurate to acknowledge that by the time of scholasticism such dissimilitude had sharply decreased, homogeneity did not result. In fact, down to our own day, churches of the East and West retain different points of view about the third person of the Trinity.[25]

A SUMMARY

We see from these observations that it could hardly have been Luke's intent to establish a didactic principle when he recorded the Pentecost event and the subsequent events in which others were Spirit-baptized. Since there was not a developed theology of the Spirit existing at that time, we must conclude that he was not attempting to convey to the future church that tongues-speech was to be considered as *normative* for persons receiving the fullness of the Spirit. It seems apparent that the *normative* idea is purely and simply a twentieth-century American notion. As has been pointed out above by Hollenweger (see footnote 2), the initial evidence doctrine is an American Pentecostal idea and is not affirmed by every Pentecostal group around the world. It is a theological construct formulated by people to explain what they had experienced. It certainly cannot be considered to be an absolute doctrine that stands above the word of God and the facts of history. Being a humanly construed concept, it must also be open to reform and adjustment in the light of a competent interpretation of the word of God.

Sound hermeneutical procedure leads us to conclude that using tongues-speech as the *primary* evidence that one has been Spirit-baptized is questionable at best. There is a biblical evidence which attests to the reality of Spirit-baptism. This we will discuss in the last section of this work.

23. Burgess, *Spirit*, 12.

24. Rusch, *Holy Spirit*, 72.

25. Ibid., 66.

9

Overdue Adjustments in Pentecostal Theology

REFLECTING ON WHAT HAS been said thus far in this work it becomes apparent that we Pentecostals have had an emphasis on the charismatic dimension of the Christian life at the expense of the ethical.

THE ETHICAL MUST BE PRIMARY

One adjustment needed in Pentecostal theology is to bring the ethical dimension of Christian life into proper relationship with the charismatic dimension. Caution must be exercised so that we do not fall into the trap of over correction. However, the ethical dimension must be considered primary.

Should you doubt the veracity of that statement I invite you to consider the most profound ethical statement ever made in this world—the cross of Jesus Christ. Alienation marked the relationship between God and humanity. The ethical nature of God demanded the cross. "While we were yet sinners Christ died for us." A moral wrong had to be made right and God took the initiative to right that wrong. Let us never forget that before the charismatic day of Pentecost came the ethical Day of Atonement, a day where wrongs were made right between God and Man. This in itself should speak volumes to us regarding the importance of the ethical in our daily living. When we attempt to place the charismatic before the ethical we are denying the very order God himself has established to rule the conduct of the Christian life.

The ethical and the charismatic must be held in a healthy, creative tension, never allowing one to eclipse the other. Ethics, without the dynamic of the charismatic, can become a dead orthodoxy or a deadening legalism. Conversely, the charismatic without the ethical becomes so much fluff, or as the Apostle has noted, an empty sound, a resounding gong, or a clanging symbol (1 Cor 13:1). Just as a gong or a cymbal becomes an irritating and ugly noise when heard in isolation, even so does the charismatic when divorced from the ethical. When the above mentioned instruments are heard within the balance, harmony, and precision of the symphony, they have meaning and lend themselves to the overall beauty of the orchestration, becoming a joy and not an irritation, a thing of beauty and not ugliness. In like manner, the charismatic, when exercised within the balance, harmony, and precision of ethical living, becomes a thing of beauty and great joy, adding to and building up the body of Christ!

In reference to 1 Corinthians 13, R. E. O. White, Principal of the Baptist Theological College of Scotland, notes that Paul enumerates the expressions of the zealous spirit that have been revered throughout Christian history, concepts essential in religion: "emotional experience, intellectual understanding, practical and energetic faith, generous philanthropy, courageous martyrdom."[1] Every one of these, insists Paul, is without meaning in the absence of the imperative of the ethical.

Lest readers think I am advocating a return to legalistic holiness, let me make clear that is the furthest thing from my intent. The cold, dead legalism of the past must rest in peace. It should not be resurrected. Modern Pentecostals were correct in their rejection of those rigid, life sapping strictures that paraded as holiness yet were more the product of fleshly efforts of works-righteousness than they were the produce of the Holy Spirit replicating the character of Christ in the believer's life. What is being advocated here is that any person or group of persons who claim to have received the fullness of the Holy Spirit and to be walking in the Spirit should be subjected to the scrutiny of the ethical demands set forth in the word of God and be expected to exhibit expressions of ethical living in the practicality of every day relationships, instead of touting their spiritual gifts.

This adjustment is sorely needed in our day. When Pentecostals are sometimes noted not so much for their charismatic expressions as for their lack of character, something is surely amiss. When fickleness is more apparent than faithfulness, there is something tragically eccentric in those lives. When confusion replaces confession, sin lies at the door. When the *material* becomes more important than *people*, there is a sickness present that robs anything charismatic of any meaning whatsoever. The spirit

---

1. White, *Biblical Ethics*, 158.

of worldliness that has invaded the modern church is not the result of deserting the old concepts of holiness. Rather, it is the result of failing to pursue the moral theology that would have provided the basis upon which to build character, faithfulness, and integrity.

We have rightly escaped the cocoon of legalistic holiness, but what have we replaced it with? At least legalistic holiness did furnish the basis for a semblance of ethical concerns. Now we seem to float in a vacuum of confused indifference, insisting that because we can speak in tongues we are Spirit-filled people and have need of little. This thinking is Corinthian in nature and is precisely that which Paul struggled against at Corinth in his day. It is this spirit against which he directs his energies, in the power of the Holy Spirit, in his letters to that church. The whole of the first letter is a treatise on Christian ethics, which were sorely needed in the Corinthian community. Chapters 10 through 14 contain Paul's argument that the charismatic is meaningless without the ethical dimension of the Christian life. Positioned in the middle of these chapters is Paul's great ode to love. That is not accidental! It is intentional! For love is the catalyst out of which all true ethical concerns rise and it is the empowerment from which every ethical consideration comes to fruition.

Michael Harper, commenting on this condition, observes:

> There are some features of pentecostalism which suggest that love has not been one of its strong points. Its fissiparous tendencies are well known. It has split into innumerable Churches and groups, often competing with one another. Its unity is fragile. Its attacks on the other Churches and its unwillingness to co-operate with them is a feature of its life.[2]

Though what Harper has stated holds true for a large percentage of the Christian church and not merely us Pentecostals, we still must listen carefully to an outsider's observations of conditions that do, indeed, exist. The time has come for us Pentecostals to become concerned about quality of character and with that aspect of Christian living that will cultivate the character of Jesus Christ in believers. Not merely through pulpit verbiage, but through intentional formation of the likeness of Jesus Christ in believers via example and discipling on the part of Christian leaders that insists the ethical dimension of the Christian life is that which gives substance and meaning to all else that we do as Christians.

2. Harper, *Love Affair*, 161–62.

A perceptive perusal of Holy Scripture will inform the open mind that the paramount concern of God for the church and humanity is that the ethical dimension of life be attended to with great care and concern. This care and concern for the ethical, in the maintenance of right relationships between God and humanity, between person and person (which is the true expression of holiness), becomes a primary consideration in the attempt to formulate a new evidential construct for Spirit-baptism.

WHO IS CHARISMATIC?

A second adjustment concerns our ideas relative to what constitutes charismatic experience. At present we hold too narrow a view in this regard. The concept of the charismatic is rooted in the Greek word *chairo*. From this root derive a family of words: *charis, charism, charisma, charismata*, and our word charismatic. These all speak of grace, and in the New Testament context they speak of God's grace.[3] Paul informs us that it is through this grace that we are saved (Eph 2:8.) He further insists that this grace has become the very element in which we have our being (Rom 5:1–2.) The charisms of the Spirit are gifts of grace. Grace weaves its way throughout the salvific process. We encounter it at every turn. It is foundational, yet grace is our ever present companion, granting to the believer both the unmerited favor of God and his divine enablement, empowering us by his Spirit to accomplish his will. Anyone one who has turned to God through Christ has become a part of the people of the charism. Paul insists on this: "If anyone does not have the Spirit of Christ, he does not belong to Christ" (Rom 8:9). Since grace is part and parcel of our salvation, and since that charis has brought to us the presence of the Spirit and the charisms of the Spirit, which are the charismata, it is only logical to conclude that every child of God is charismatic.

Paul informs us that each believer has been given grace, and he states this in the context of the gifting of every believer (Rom 12:6.) Being charismatic means that one has been born from above, is indwelt by the Holy Spirit, and has available the empowerment of the Spirit for holy living and service, whether one has appropriated this grace or not. To limit this concept to mean that one must have spoken in tongues or manifested one or another of the charisms of the Spirit is untenable on the basis of an exegetical perusal of the matter. All Christians are charismatic, whether

3. Kittel and Friedrich, *Theological Dictionary*, 9:394–96.

they are aware of it or agree to it. It is simply a matter of fact that cannot be denied. It is the nature of the Christian to be charismatic. God has freely given to his people his charis (grace), and it is that charis that causes one to be charismatic, in whatever manner God chooses to express it in the life of a particular believer.

It must be acknowledged that some believers seem to have a greater propensity toward the charismata than do others. There are Christians who freely express the charisms of the Spirit in full spectrum, while others may express only those charisms that are not immediately observable. Labeling the former as being charismatic and denying such a status to the latter can only come from a limited concept of the ministry of God's grace in the midst of the life of the church.

THE NEED FOR SPIRITUAL DISCERNMENT

The third adjustment needed in Pentecostal theology is a recognition of the need to emphasize the charism of discernment. We are rather naive in this day relative to manifestations of the Spirit. We have the tendency to accept any and all such expressions as being of the Spirit, with little concern that they might be the product of the flesh or, possibly, of demons. Not all demonic manifestation should be expected to be expressed in an obvious manner. We must remember that our adversary also comes as an angel of light.-

Charismatic expression should be subjected to mature discernment on the part of the whole church but especially by the leadership of the church. We must not be so eager to place our *Spirit-filled* stamp on people that we fail to exercise true discernment of spirits. I am afraid that in our eagerness to see people experience Spirit-baptism we may prematurely declare some to be Spirit-filled without a full accounting of the evidence. Again, the ethical dimension of the Christian life must be held to be primary in these considerations. Regardless of any charismatic expression identified as the first verifiable evidence of the event, we must insist that the life of such a person begin to produce the peaceable fruit of righteousness, that is, a life that expresses the ethical dimension of Christian living, the character of Jesus Christ. This must be an *expected* development in the life of the Spirit-filled.

This will take a great deal of wisdom, discernment, and a dependence upon the Spirit.

PART FOUR

The Ultimate Evidence

10

The Pauline Evidential Construct

IT SEEMS LOGICAL THAT if Scripture intended to convey to the Church that glossolalia is to be understood as the *primary evidence* of Spirit-baptism, literature as important to Christian theology as the Pauline corpus would contain a didactic strain that would confirm such a notion.

We would strain credulity to produce the concept from Paul. Indeed, though the apostle affirms the validity of glossolalia, he does not elevate it to the position of *primary* in evidential considerations, and he does repeatedly emphasize the absolute necessity that the believer embrace in day to day living the ethical demands placed upon them by the agape of the cross.

In reference to Paul's thought on the ethical dimension of the Spirit, W. D. Davies notes:

> While it is true that it was not Paul who ethicized the Spirit as we have maintained, on the other hand it is clear that he did bring order into a very confused apprehension of the activity of the Spirit, which seems to have prevailed in the thought of the primitive Church ... evidently the situation that confronted Paul at Corinth, for example, was that glossolaly and ecstasy and other marks of enthusiasm in the life of the Church were given a status equal to that of the moral as expressions of the Spirit; and we cannot doubt that it was Paul who isolated the moral aspect of the activity of the Spirit and brought order into the confusion of popular Christian thought; it was he who introduced the idea that *agape* was a more excellent way.[1]

---

1. Davies, *Paul*, 220–21; see also chapter 8, "The Old and New Obedience: I. The Lord the Spirit," in its entirety for an astute assessment of Paul's understanding of the person and work of the Spirit.

Turning, then, to Paul's writings we discover that it is entirely possible that the instruction he gives the Corinthian church relative to glossolalia is his attempt to combat the influence of the mystery religions on the converts who came to Christ. As was pointed out in chapter 1, the mysteries placed an inordinate emphasis on speaking with tongues and viewed this phenomenon as being a clear *sign* that the tongues speaker was, indeed, possessed by the gods. It may be that Paul is making an oblique reference to this notion in 1 Corinthians 14:22ff and is endeavoring to correct the Corinthians' faulty thinking in that regard.

Paul is discussing here the value of tongues and prophecy, and while he does insist that no one be forbidden to speak in tongues, it is clear that he understands prophecy to be more desirable for the gathered church than glossolalia. In his words: "Tongues, then, are a sign, not for believers, but for unbelievers" (1 Cor 14:22). This is one of the difficult statements of Paul that has rarely been understood.

Analysis of four key Greek words used in this passage reveals the strong possibility that Paul is actually referring to the practice and thought of the mysteries relative to glossolalia. He employs the words *saimeion* and *apistos* in verse 22, and in verse 23 he uses *mainesthea* and *propheteia*.

First, *saimeion* translates into English as "sign." Karl Rengstorf informs us that *saimeion* is used in a variety of ways, the context or the author's consistent usage usually determining its meaning in a particular instance. Traditionally *saimeion* does not have theological reference but anthropological. The word is functional and technical even when its object is a moral or religious truth. However, Rengstorf insists, "Even here it has nothing to do with revelation in the religious sense."[2] It not only bears connotations of optical perception but also denotes acoustical impression—hearing and what is heard.[3] Basically, *saimeion* means "an indication." Paul, according to Rengstorf, uses *saimeion* in the traditional sense of the word.[4]

Second, *apistos* refers to the unbeliever, the pagan, the non-Christian.[5] F. F. Bruce also identifies the *apistos* as the non-Christian.[6] It is entirely

2. Rengstorf, "saimeion," 204.

3. Ibid., 202–3.

4. Ibid., 258.

5. Bultmann, "apistos," 204–5.

6. Bruce, *I & II Corinthians*, 133.

possible that Paul's intent in this statement bears the following connotation: "Tongues may serve as a sign for pagans that they are filled with the spirit of their gods; however, for us Christians that is a false belief." Allowing that the influence of the mysteries is present in the Corinthian church, a thesis with probable historicity, this interpretation makes a great deal of sense.

Third, the language employed in verse 23 also indicates that Paul may be continuing his oblique reference to the practices of the Hellenistic religions. There he advises the Corinthians that if unbelievers come into the worship service and hear them all speaking in tongues, "will they not say that you are out of your mind?" This is exactly the notion expressed by observers of participants in the Hellenistic mysteries when the participants were in a state of ecstasy—in fact, the mysteries concept of ecstasy or enthusiasm connotes that one has left the state of rationality and, in this sense, is out of one's mind and in total possession by the gods. This was known as being *mainesthai*.

Herbert Preisker has observed that for the Greeks *mainesthai* ("out-of-your-mind") "is not just a pathological expression. It is not a malady or the result of wrong instruction. To be in ecstasy to the point of frenzy is a divine transportation from customary states. It is a strongly affirmed religious phenomenon. Even a god, Dionysus, is a *mainomenos* in *Hom. Il.*, 6, 132, and the supreme blessing of this frenzied god is to draw his followers into the same *mainesthai*."[7] Preisker also notes:

> Plato describes the blessing of the divine sent madness (*mainia*, *mainesthai*), which gives different insights from the knowledge acquired by the more sober. He points to the *Pythia*, the priestesses of Dodona, and divinely inspired poets. *Mainesthai* can also be used for Bacchic possession and divine rapture. (Bacchus is another name for the god Dionysus.)[8]

Mainesthai refers to the psychic state that a *believer* participating in a religious ceremony reaches in ecstasy, which observers would term being "out of your mind." It is possible to understand verse 23 to mean that when the Corinthian church is all speaking in tongues they resemble participants in the mystery rites appearing to be *mainesthai*.

7. Preisker, "mainesthai," 360.
8. Ibid.

Fourth, Paul compares the impact of glossolalia and prophecy on the believer (14:24, 25), emphasizing that prophecy convinces the non-Christian. Gerhard Friedrich avers that "prophecy is the revelation and testimony of Jesus Christ; it is the Word of God."[9] Friedrich further notes that for Paul, the prophet's "chief mark is the Word which God has given him to proclaim. The prophet in the Pauline congregation is not the seer but the recipient and preacher of the Word. . . . For the prophet the secret counsels of God are revealed, and he declares them to the community through his preaching."[10] British Pentecostal Donald Gee appears to affirm this idea when he comments: "The guiding mark of prophetical ministry is that it carries a *message* from God."[11] Gee contends that the task of the Christian prophet is not unlike that of the Hebrew prophet: "In its essentials prophesying remains the same.[12] Prophetic preaching, empowered by the Spirit, becomes the convincing factor for the unbeliever. In this preaching the unbeliever hears the voice of God and falls down and worships him.

It is entirely possible, then, to interpret verse 23 in the sense that Paul is making further reference to the Hellenistic religions' practice of glossolalia, with the accompanying ecstatic frenzy, and that prophecy, a word from God, as understandable speech is a convincing indicator that *God is really among you!* John Ruef comments on this phrase: "*God is really among you*: This is a stereotyped confession in the biblical tradition. It indicates the acceptance of one deity as opposed to another."[13]

What Paul appears to be saying to the Corinthians is that the convincing factor for the unbeliever, who is already accustomed to hearing glossolalia in the Hellenistic religions, is hearing the proclamation of the word of God in the demonstration of the Spirit and of power. In addition, verse 24 indicates that the charism "the word of knowledge" may also be involved, for Paul indicates that "the secrets of his heart will be laid bare." Certainly this could be a reference to this charism of the Spirit exposing the unbeliever's need for the Savior, causing him to fall down and worship God as he exclaims, "*God is really among you!*"

9. Kittel and Friedrich, *Theological Dicitionary*, 6:850.

10. Ibid.

11. Gee, *Spiritual Gifts*, 54.

12. Ibid.

13. Ruef, *Paul's First Letter*, 151.

This hypothesis is reinforced when we observe that Paul makes explicit reference to their former religious practices in 1 Corinthians 12:1–2: "Now about spiritual gifts, brothers, I do not want you to be ignorant. *You know that when you were pagans*, somehow or other you were influenced and led astray to mute idols" (emphasis mine). Paul then proceeds to set forth instruction regarding the proper use of the gifts of the Holy Spirit, including glossolalia, thereby indicating that the Corinthians were being influenced, in some respects, by the pagan mind set and practice.

It is not merely happenstance that Paul positions what we have come to refer to as his "ode" or hymn to love" between chapters 12 and 14. He is making a categorical statement in so doing. The *ultimate evidence* that one is filled with the Spirit of God is the concrete expression of agape in the practicality of everyday living. The charismatic, void of the ethical, is insufficient. In point of fact, Paul states that it means *nothing*.

W. D. Davies has noted that "for Paul the whole of the Christian life in its ethical no less than in its 'ecstatic' aspects is the expression of the activity of the Holy Spirit."[14]

It is significant that Paul begins this statement with a reference to the glossolalic phenomenon: "If I speak in the tongues of men and of angels, but have not love, I am only a resounding gong or a clanging cymbal" (1 Cor 13:1). Marcus Bach informs us that in the Eleusinian and Dionysian festivals much of the tongues-speaking resembled "sounding brass and tinkling cymbal."[15] Paul continues his discourse with the statement, "If I have the gift of prophecy and can fathom all mysteries and all knowledge . . . but have not love, I am nothing" (1 Cor 13:2). The fact that prophecy, mystery, and knowledge were all an integral part of the Hellenistic religions reinforces the supposition that Paul is, indeed, making oblique reference to these religions in this passage.[16]

Paul's emphasis seems to be that the only reliable evidence of being possessed by (filled with) the Holy Spirit is the ultimate evidence of the active expression of agape, God's love, in the concreteness of life, not these

14. Davies, *Paul*, 217.

15. Bach, *Inner Ecstasy*, 72–73.

16. The accepted position of many New Testament scholars is that these notions are the result of a pre-gnostic or gnostic influence in the Corinthian church. However, as H. Wayne House has ably demonstrated, it is more probable that these ideas come from the mystery religions that were prevalent in Corinth and valued these very things (see House, "Mystery Religions," 138).

manifestations that were endorsed by the mysteries as evidence of divine possession. This love, observes Paul, produces in the life of the believer the very qualities that the Corinthians so obviously lacked, that is, the greater gifts he alludes to in verse 29 of chapter 12. These greater gifts are based in and rise out of God's agape. He identifies them in chapter 13, verses 4 through 7: love is patient, kind, does not envy, does not boast, is not proud, is not rude, is not self-seeking, not easily angered, keeps no record of wrongs, does not delight in evil, rejoices in the truth, always protects, always trusts, always hopes, always perseveres. This love never fails. This love influences the quality of human relationships, that is, how one person relates to and treats another person. Paul views this action as being anchored in, and an expression of, the agape of the cross.

Don Evans, a Welsh Pentecostal, notes that embedded in 1 Corinthians 13 we find the fruit of the Spirit that Paul enumerates in Galatians 5:22. "What was lacking in the Corinthian church," states Evans, "was love; a lack in the character of the people, and with love, so many correlates of personality that together make up the spiritual man. What is it that marks out the spiritual man from others? Is it charismata or character? The Bible answer is quite definitive and unequivocal, it is character! It is the man in whose life the character of Jesus is reproduced who is the spiritual man."[17]

The love Paul describes to the Corinthians is vastly different from their behavior, as anyone can perceive by reading the two letters of Paul written to them. Paul seems to be asking, Do you believe that the evidence of possession by the gods of your old religions is an adequate evidence that you are now filled with God's Spirit? His answer is, no! It is totally inadequate! There is one standard by which to measure the reality of your experience, and that is the presence of God's agape at work in your life, which will produce in you all of the things that are now, by nature, foreign to your behavior, that is, the very character of Jesus Christ. If you are truly filled with God's Spirit, you will manifest much more than speaking in tongues or prophecy or knowledge. You will evidence the concrete expression of volitional love (agape), which does the right things, regardless! That is the ethical way, the more excellent way!

---

17. Evans, "The Spiritual Man." Dr. Evans is Professor of Philosophy at the University of Wales, Swansea.

The qualities of character that Paul enumerates in these verses of scripture are qualities that are foreign to the human heart. People do not live this way of their own accord. It is impossible for them to do so. Only the Holy Spirit can produce the genuine manifestations of God's love in the life of the believer—to love selflessly, unconditionally, unmotivated, and spontaneously. The flesh cannot replicate them, nor can the demonic imitate them. The pressures of life reveal the presence of true agape and its correlates and expose the counterfeit. True agape will stand the test of these tensions. The mask of the false will crack and crumble under such pressures and will reveal the true nature of the masquerade. Only that which is produced by the Spirit of God (agape) can pass the testing of the realities of life; this is the *ultimate evidence* that one is filled with the Holy Spirit. What Paul is emphasizing here is the ethical side of the Christian way of life. Oliver Barclay, in observing Paul's emphasis and concern for the ethical dimension of the Christian life, comments:

> Paul is offering neither a "Love God and do what you like" view of the Christian life nor a new Christian legalism. He makes it plain that his overall rule is love, but love which is worked out in intelligent application of the known will of God as outlined in the Ten Commandments, understood as Jesus taught us to understand them."[18]

Barclay reminds us that the ethical concerns of Paul and the other New Testament writers are neither a crass legalism nor a permissive situationalism, "It is neither hard and brittle (legalism) nor soft and pliable (situationalism), but tough like steel. New Testament morality comes to us as revealed guidelines with the authority of God for our acceptance, but also for careful outworking in our own different situations."[19]

Henlee Barnette instructs us that, "Like Jesus, Paul presents no code of laws for the Christian life. Rather, he lays down basic principles of behavior which the individual and the church can discover and apply in moral decision and action." "Love," insists Barnette, "is the chief moral principle of Paul's ethics. In his thought, love—not law—is the indwelling and all-embracing ethical force of the Christian life."[20]

18. Barclay, *Intellect and Beyond*, 28.
19. Ibid., 35.
20. Barnette, *Christian Ethics*, 71.

The charismata are indeed a part of God's purpose for his people, however, the charismata are to be balanced by the fruit of the Spirit and if not, then there is strong reason to question the validity of what appears, on the surface, to be charismatic. Michael Harper correctly notes, "Love always leads to the keeping of the commandments, and the keeping of the commandments is the way to abide in God's love. Love is both the fruit of the Holy Spirit and the root of obedience."[21]

I suspect that much of what passes today as charismatic or pentecostal may be no more than the mere product of the flesh. Dressed, to be sure, in that which passes for the finery of the charisms of the Spirit, these pseudo-charismata are devoid of any real moral or ethical value and therefore, under the judgment of the word of God given through Paul, amount to nothing.

Though a full treatment of Paul's views regarding the ethical and the charismatic is a work unto itself, here, I do desire to look at two more instances of his concern for the ethical. In 2 Corinthians 8, Paul is nudging the Corinthians to exhibit a Christ-like attitude toward those less fortunate than themselves. He holds before them the Macedonian churches as an example of unfeigned love. Even in the midst of their own need these churches responded in practical love, meeting the needs of fellow believers. Paul insists that he is not commanding the Corinthians' participation; however, by requesting it he states that he desires "to test the sincerity of your love by comparing it with the earnestness of others" (8:8). What Paul is calling them to is the practice of Christian ethics (agape), demonstrated by their willingness to give to the needs of others. The heart of Paul's concern for this church, in all of what he writes to them, is that they learn to demonstrate the indwelling presence of God's Spirit by concrete ethical behavior, for this is the true test of the abiding presence of Christ in the believer's life.

Romans 13:8–10 also expresses Paul's concern for the ethical. There he insists that the Christian should owe no one anything, "except the continuing debt to love one another, for he who loves his fellow man has fulfilled the law." All commandments, insists Paul, "are summed up in this one rule: Love your neighbor as yourself. Love does no harm to its neighbor. Therefore love is the fulfillment of the law."

---

21. Harper, *Love Affair*, 53.

It would be sheer arrogance for contemporary Christians, Pentecostals and Charismatics in particular, to ignore the implications of these statements of Paul. Love is primary! Everything else falls under the judgment of agape! If it does not pass the governing criteria of agape it must be declared invalid, ineffective, and nothing. The agape of the cross rules as *primary* over everything else in the Christian's life.

A perusal of these and the more than forty other instances of Paul's teaching on agape must convince us that, for the apostle, *the ethical manifestation of the Holy Spirit is primary*. There is no greater evidential phenomenon! Everything else is subsumed under love and must pass the test of love if it is to gain the credibility of being a product of the Holy Spirit.

Davies has noted: "It is the fact that for Paul Christianity is essentially 'pneumatic' (that he interprets Christianity through the category of the Spirit) that makes it inevitable that he should also give greater significance to the ethical aspect of the pneumatic life."[22]

---

22. Davies, *Paul*, 220.

11

The Biblical Evidential Paradigm

JOHN DID NOT SAY, God is charismatic. Jesus did not say that glossolalia would mark his disciples. James did not say that pure, undefiled religion would be found in charismatic experiences. Nor did Paul say that the greatest of these is ecstatic utterance. All of the above mentioned statements rivet our attention on one thing—the biblical evidential paradigm that we seek. The witness of the New Testament in its entirety presents this in a consistent manner. This is the ultimate evidence of the Spirit-filled life.

What John did say was, "God is love" (1 John 4:8b). Jesus said, "All men will know you are my disciples if you love one another" (John 13:35). James insisted, "Religion that God our Father accepts as pure and faultless is this: to look after orphans and widows in their distress and to keep oneself from being polluted by the world" (James 1:27). Paul's declaration was that love is primary: "*The greatest of these is love*" (1 Cor 13:13).

Leon Morris notes that there is a great deal about love in the Old Testament and that "understanding the meaning of love is essential to understanding the Old Testament." Relative to the New Testament, he further observes, "It is scarcely possible to write about the New Testament without noticing that love is one of its most important topics—if not the most important of them."[1]

In this work I will not attempt to labor through the Old Testament emphasis on love but rather limit the considerations to New Testament concerns. However, it should be noted here that the Old Testament concept of *hesed* appears to be the equivalent to the New Testament idea of agape. *Hesed*, according to Dom R. Sorg, "is the Old Testament revelation of St. John's: 'God is charity' (1 John 4:16), inasmuch as this connotes God's

---

1. Morris, *Testaments*, 4, 5.

own way of loving and the secret motive of all His thinking and willing and acting."[2] We must not, then, think that the New Testament notion of God's love is something new in Christian thought (though it undoubtedly came into sharper focus and full development in the New Testament). Rather, we must understand it to be an extension of the Old Testament idea, reinterpreted in the light of the revelation of God in Christ.

Due to the misuse and abuse of the word love in the English vocabulary, it is necessary, at this juncture, to define what love means in the present context and the source from which that definition has derived.

Love, as used in this work, makes reference to that quality of love the New Testament writers determined to be God's love. Since this type of love was a new concept to the world of their day, they elected to adapt a little used Greek word and invest it with new meaning. That word is agape.[3] Agape is used in the gospels as well as the epistles to identify the love that proceeds from God alone. The concept comes to its highest and most complete development in the Pauline corpus.[4]

Anders Nygren, speaking of the agape motif in the life and teaching of Jesus, comments:

> This idea is not one among other equally important ideas; it is *the fundamental motif of Christianity,* which sets its stamp on everything else. It is the idea of Agape that hallmarks the new way of fellowship with God which Christianity brings, and the idea of Agape that characterizes its new ethic and turns the old commandment of love into a "new commandment" with a specific Christian content.[5]

This love becomes the determinative factor in the matter of ethical questions and decisions. What is right and what is wrong? As I write this I am aboard a Boeing 727 cruising at 30,000 feet en route from Seattle to Los Angeles. There were certain absolutes with which the pilots of this

---

2. Sorg, *Hesed,* 53.

3. Barth, *Church Dogmatics,* 177–78.

4. Nygren, *Agape and Eros,* 109–45. (Nygren's brilliant and monumental work on the Christian concept of agape examines the development of the agape motif in Paul's theology. I am satisfied that Nygren has made a strong case for his assertion that Paul has brought the agape idea to its fullest development, that he did not merely borrow the concept but actually brought it to a point of completion, accurately reflecting the views of Jesus. The concept is stated in his uniquely Pauline way, yet is faithful to the fundamental religious and ethical motif found in the teachings of Jesus.)

5. Ibid., 108 (emphasis mine).

aircraft *had* to comply, in order for this composite of aluminum, plastic, and humanity to lift off *terra firma*. There are, as well, absolutes the pilots must adhere to if they intend to keep the craft in the air, just as there are other absolutes they must honor in order to provide a safe landing at Los Angeles International Airport. There are right ways and there are wrong ways, and only those who respect the right way to do a thing will do it effectively. The pilots of this craft will assure you that there is no *other* way to take off, fly, and land this aircraft than the way in which they have been trained.

It amazes me that intelligent people can acknowledge the absolutes that govern nature while at the same time denying any moral criteria that might be labeled *absolute*. In dealing with the question of what is right and what is wrong, the secularist of our day would argue that the question of moral absolutes is a moot point. Since (they claim) there are no moral absolutes to govern human activity, why ask the question?

However, as evangelical Christians we are compelled to grapple with the question of moral integrity. The basis offered by the secularist upon which one *might* construct an ethical system is wholly inadequate for the evangelical believer. The Evangelical insists that there are answers to ethical questions. We reject the Fletcherian notion that there are no longer black and white categories in moral concerns and that one must wrestle for answers in a nebulous grey. Such an idea leaves vacuous holes in any moral system.

Joseph Fletcher spawned an ethical system holding to no absolutes, save one—*love*.[6] However, Fletcher's concept of a self-seeking, self-fulfilling love is far removed from the idea of love revealed to humanity by God the Father through the incarnate Son, Jesus Christ. This love is the diametric opposite of the erotic notion posited by Fletcher. Agape is a self-giving, self-sacrificing love that deems the welfare of others to be primary in every human relationship. Fletcher's *Situation Ethics* fail exactly at that point. The inverted, egocentricity of his notion is the very thing Scripture identifies as sin. On the other hand, Jesus emphatically insists

---

6. For an excellent critique of Fletcher's *Situation Ethics,* see Harper, *Love Affair,* 63–183. Though Fletcher appeals to Christian agape as the absolute in his ethical system, his version of agape bears more of the appearance of *eros* than of God's love. Nygren addresses this confusion of eros and agape in his work. Fletcher has made the grievous error that has been made by a multitude of religious thinkers, attempting to syncretize agape and eros, incompatible opposites.

that the greatest moral or ethical demonstration one can express is laying down one's life for a friend (John 15:13).

Agape, God's love, is the volitional action produced in human behavior by the Holy Spirit that does the right thing regardless of the motions of the soul. It does not rise out of informed *feelings*, rather, it proceeds from thoughtful, willed actions intended to benefit and profit another with no thought of reciprocation or personal benefit. It is this fruit of grace that serves as the bedrock of all Christian living. It is not dependent upon any part of Abraham Maslow's hierarchy of needs. Maslow's observations are valid, but they are not the motivating factor in any expression of agape. Agape is not prompted in any way by fleshly desire, but it is wholly produced in the life of the believer by the indwelling Spirit of God. By setting forth love as the *ultimate evidence* of the Spirit-filled life, I am not proposing the type of love conceived by Enlightenment thought, as embodied in Fletcherian ethics. Nor do I refer to the erotic notion of Greek philosophy, a notion that appears to form the basis of the Fletcherian idea of love. Rather, I mean that spontaneous and unmotivated love that issues from God and is witnessed to in the gospel tradition and the epistles of the various New Testament writers, particularly those of Paul.

When speaking of the ethical I do not mean legal. Paul effectively divorced Christian ethics from the system of the law and united ethics with what Nygren calls *the Agape of the Cross*. Agape, which forms the new ethical base for the people of God, rises out of the very nature of God ("God is love," 1 John 4:16) and not from his law given through Moses.

R. E. O. White has correctly perceived that Paul posits a new moral principle: "Paul declares that neither heredity nor ritual (nor any lack of either) really matters: but faith, made an operative principle of moral life by love."[7] As Nygren insists that agape is "the fundamental motif of Christianity" and that it "characterizes its new ethic," so White emphatically notes that Paul is unfailingly loyal to Christ's insight here:

> He who loves his neighbor has fulfilled the law: the commandments, You shall not commit adultery, You shall not kill, You shall not steal, You shall not covet, or any other commandment, are summed up in the sentence, You shall love your neighbor as yourself. Love does no wrong to a neighbor: therefore love is the fulfilling of the law. (Romans 13:8–10)[8]

7. White, *Biblical Ethics*, 157; see also Gal 6:2, 5:14.
8. Ibid., 157–58.

"The supremacy of love," White further observes, "emerges equally clear when Paul echoes the baptismal catechesis" in his instruction to the churches and is seen as well in his hymn to love, 1 Corinthians 13:[9]. White sees in Paul the catching up of all that is ethical and moral and the binding of it to his understanding of what God's agape actually means and does.

Commenting on this idea, he notes:

> Compared with the endless elaboration and complexity of most moral systems that rest upon codes of law and casuistry, this *formal simplification* of moral obligation into one overriding precept, of active, universal, persistent and undiscourageable goodwill, offers immense clarity to the earnest mind and relief to the scrupulous conscience.[10]

Nygren traces the growth of the agape motif from the gospels through Paul, demonstrating the development of the motif in Christian thought. The signal factor evident in his study is that agape, with its ensuing ethical behavior produced in the believer, as a revelation of the love of God through man, is spontaneous and unmotivated. In other words, God's love to man, as seen best in the incarnation and the cross of Christ, and God's love through man, as seen best in the Spirit-filled, Spirit-led believer's social relationships, needs no stimulus either in the keeping of the legal requirements of the law or in some supposed inherent value in the human person. As Nygren has correctly observed, "We have, therefore no longer any reason to ask about either the best or worse qualities of those who are the objects of Divine love. To the question, Why does God love? there is only one right answer: Because it is His nature to love."[11]

One of the most poignant statements in Scripture is recorded by John in his gospel: "For God so loved the world that he gave his one and only Son, that who ever believes in him shall not perish but have eternal life" (3:16).

THE AGAPE OF THE CROSS

In what Nygren calls *the Agape of the Cross*, we see the highest expression of ethical behavior known to man. There was nothing compelling God to kenotic action, neither in the creation of humanity nor in the incarnation of the eternal Logos in human form. What God did at Calvary was wholly

9. Ibid., 158.

10. Ibid., 160.

11. Nygren, *Agape and Eros*, 75.

spontaneous and unmotivated. In fact, Paul informs us that "while we were still sinners, Christ died for us" (Rom 5:8b). He owed us nothing! He simply loved us! Jesus apprized his hearers on one occasion that agape is primary and a commandment, not an option. "My command is this: Love each other as I have loved you. Greater Love has no man than this, that one lay down his life for his friends" (John 15:12–13). This was not mere rhetoric on Christ's part. In the incarnation he had already laid down his life in a manner that we cannot, in our finiteness, ever comprehend. He was also looking toward the cross and all the ignominy that it entailed. He was insisting that those who would follow him live in the same self-sacrificing manner. This is how true love, God's love, expresses itself. This is the highest form of ethical behavior for any person.

Geddes MacGregor comments,

> To say that the biblical God is love is to say that his creation is an act, not of self-expression but of self-limitation. For the biblical God, being ontologically perfect himself as well as sovereign over and independent of his creatures, could have nowhere to go by way of expansion. He could have no ambitions to fulfill or goals to attain or projects to promote either for his aggrandizement or for his betterment. The only way he could go in his creative act would be a way of self-limitation, self-emptying, self-abnegation. That is what *agape* would entail.[12]

Earlier in his gospel John records Jesus's identifying the ultimate evidence of belonging to his kingdom and its king—being Spirit-filled and Spirit-led. Again it is couched in the form of a commandment: "A new commandment I give you: Love one another. As I have loved you, so you must love one another. All men will know that you are my disciples if you love one another" (John 13:34–35). Peter's response is probably indicative of our dullness and our callous attitude toward this commandment. Rather than asking how one could love as Jesus did, Peter completely ignores what Jesus has just said and questions him regarding his words, "Where I am going, you cannot come" (John 13:33). However, it is unmistakable that Jesus is instructing his apostles that the hallmark, the primary evidence of the Spirit's presence in a believer's life, will be agape in action.

---

12. MacGregor, *Theology of Love*, 19.

On another occasion, recorded by Matthew, Jesus was teaching on love as it is expressed in forgiveness and the procedure one should follow in maintaining right relationships through love. Peter responds to this teaching with the question, "Lord, how many times shall I forgive my brother when he sins against me? Up to seven times?" (Matt 18:21). Jesus's response to Peter's query was that one's forgiveness should be immeasurable; the 470 times he speaks of is figurative and not to be taken literally. This kind of love is extremely costly to those who practice it. It costs one's very life. It requires that one truly lay down one's life for one's friends. It places *the ethical as primary* over any charismatic concern. Indeed, it is only as one maintains a life of righteousness (right relationships, horizontally as well as vertically) that any charismatic expression of the Christian life has substance and meaning.

It is of great significance that John, in his first epistle, identifies the biblical paradigm of love, ties it to the evidence that one belongs to Christ, and states that the proof of the fact is obedience to Christ's commands. "The man who says, 'I know him,' but does not do what he commands is a liar, and the truth is not in him. But if anyone obeys his word, God's love is truly made complete in him. This is how we know we are in him: Whoever claims to live in him must walk as Jesus did" (1 John 2:3–6). In the latter part of chapter 2, John again insists that obedience to the law of love is the evidence of belonging to Christ and reflecting his life. "If you know that he is righteous, you know that everyone who does what is right has been born of him" (1 John 2:29).

Again, in chapter 3, John reinforces what he has said relative to the evidence of being in Christ. "We know that we have passed from death to life, because we love our brothers. Anyone who does not love remains in death" (1 John 3:14–15). Immediately following this declaration he makes this statement: "This is how we know what love is: Jesus Christ laid down his life for us. And we ought to lay down our lives for our brothers" (1 John 3:16). John then illustrates what he means by laying down one's life for one's brother, that is, meeting whatever need that brother might have at a given moment. John's particular example is of one who has material possessions yet ignores a brother's need. "How," questions John, "can the love of God be in him?" (1 John 3:17b). He then exhorts his readers to love, not merely with words, but with actions and truth. All of this is set in the context of love—agape, God's love. "This then," declares John, "is how we know that we belong to the truth, and how we set our hearts at rest in his presence" (1 John 3:19). This is the concrete expression of ethical action, and John calls it agape.

Chapter 4 continues this vital theme. John cannot seem to stay away from it. It is in this chapter that agape is brought to its highest moment, when he declares, "God is love. Whoever lives in love lives in God, and God in him" (1 John 4:16b).

Nygren states that here we find the development of the primitive Christian idea of agape at its apex, observing that "All the essential points of the New Testament doctrine of Agape are reproduced in the Johannine writings, though John takes us a stage further by his identification of agape in its final form."[13]

SUMMARY

The objection could be raised, at this point, that the above scriptures are not referring to Spirit-baptism, rather, they speak of the consequence of being in Christ through the new birth. That would be begging the point. One cannot separate the work of the Spirit in regeneration from his consummate work as he comes in his fullness into a believer's life. That there can be a subsequent work of the Spirit in the life of the believer is not the point to be made here. I would affirm that there are probably *many* subsequent works of the Spirit in a believer's life. Paul exhorts believers to seek a continuing fullness of the Spirit, and so we must. However, it must be recognized that it is inconsistent in logic and reality, as well as with Scripture, to dichotomize the presence of the Spirit in the believer's life. Either he is there or he is not. (See the comments in chapter 5 relative to the indwelling of the Spirit.) Paul insists in Romans 8:9b "If anyone does not have the Spirit of Christ, he does not belong to Christ." This is the new birth. The Spirit has come to take up residence in the person's life. He is there, not in part, but in everything that he is! The believer may not yet know how to *release* the Spirit through his life (this release is what I would term the baptism with the Spirit), but nevertheless, the Spirit is present at that moment in all that he can ever be for the believer.

Prior to the above statement, Paul informs us that it is the Holy Spirit who brings to the believer's heart the agape of God. "God has poured out his love into our hearts by the Holy Spirit, whom he has given us" (Rom 5:5b). Paul knows of no *special* event, other than the new birth, that marks

13. Nygren, *Agape and Eros*, 149.

the coming of the Spirit into one's being. Though he claims to speak in tongues more than any of the Corinthians, we find no claim on his part that one does this as the evidence that one has received the Holy Spirit. Paul posits love, the same love that he states God has poured into our hearts, as the ultimate evidence that one has received the fullness of the Spirit.

The New Testament, on the whole, either explicitly or implicitly insists that agape is the *primary* evidence of the Spirit-filled life. We saw this in the teachings of Jesus. It was found in the writings of Matthew, John, and James, as well as in those of Paul. The overwhelming consensus of the New Testament witness is that the expression of agape in one's life is the *primary*, the *ultimate, evidence* of the Spirit-baptized life. The expression of the charismatic in the absence of the ethical amounts to nothing!

12

Toward a Comprehensive Evidential Construct

THE VALUE AND VALIDITY of Holy Spirit produced glossolalia has never been under question in this work. Glossolalia has to be considered a given for a church born of grace (charis) and sustained by grace (charis). The church can be nothing less than charismatic, and speaking in tongues is one of the charisms of the Spirit.[1] The focus of this work has been the place of glossolalia in the dogmatics of Pentecostal theology.

My concern, throughout, has been the elevated sense with which glossolalia has been invested by Pentecostals and many Charismatics. Whether the original framers of the initial evidence doctrine intended that it be so invested is open to question. Unfortunately, we do not have records of the deliberations when this construct was first formulated and therefore do not know what the intent was in using the term "initial." The very language of the construct seems to indicate that there must have been other evidences that could have been considered as primary. Why else would they have constructed the doctrine to speak of that which was initial? The word initial essentially means occurring at the beginning. And, as Wiebe has instructed us, the sense in which this should be used by Pentecostals in a construct affirming the coming of the fullness of the Spirit in the life of the believer is as *the first verifiable evidence* and no more than that. To insist that glossolalia be considered as primary places us on very tenuous ground, biblically, theologically, hermeneutically, and epistemologically.

R. Hollis Gause (CGCT) exhibits what I deem to be the proper approach to considerations of the Spirit-filled life.[2] He insists that the pres-

---

1. "Church" is intended be understood as the church universal and not merely Pentecostal/Charismatic bodies within the church.

2. Gause, *Living in the Spirit*, 1980.

ence of the Spirit in the life of the believer brings not only the Spirit's charismatic nature but also and, primarily, the nature of his holiness.

Leon Morris insists that in the New Testament the emphasis weighs heavily upon the Spirit's holiness. In reference to the title Holy Spirit, Morris comments: "This characteristic designation, found throughout the New Testament, does not draw attention to the power of the Spirit, His greatness, or the like. For the first Christians the important thing was that He is holy. His character mattered most of all."[3]

In sum, it is more important to recognize and acknowledge the Spirit's holiness than the Spirit's charismata. In like manner, it is more important that believers manifest the holiness of the Spirit than the charismatic gifts. The ethical is primary over the charismatic.

CHRISTIANITY IS FIRST AND FOREMOST RELATIONAL

By this point in our study the perceptive person will have become aware of the fact that Christianity is first and foremost relational. The Scriptures consistently deal with relationships, either between God and humanity or between human persons. The Decalogue sets forth ten commandments from God to humans. Four of these commands are directed toward God, while the remaining six concern human relations. It is significant that God weighted these commands on the side of human relations. These were the rules that were to govern the covenant relationship both between God and his people and between human individuals. Relationships connote community. A community of people is comprised of a network of relationships. For the church, the relational pattern is first God to humanity and humanity to God. Secondly, it is person to person in the various relationships that constitute human society: parent to child, spouse to spouse, sibling to sibling, friend to friend, employer to employee, and so on.

The Godhead: The Ultimate Community

God has always governed his people through covenant. Covenant is God's ethical standard that sets forth the rules by which relationships between two or more persons are governed.

We find our model in the opening verses of Genesis. There we discover a series of statements that read, "And God said . . ." The full impact of what is being said in the Hebrew simply cannot be translated into English

3. Morris, *John*, 656.

in a few words. The Hebrew word translated "said" in this passage is *amar*. Siegfried Wagner has pointed out that *amar* has manifold meanings. In this instance, *amar* means "to say" in the sense of one person imparting information or instructions to another. *Amar* always appears in a subject/object relationship and quite often takes two objects, that is, the person or persons being addressed as well as an accusative object designating the direct object of the verb. *Amar* always expresses a personal relationship; it is used to denote communication between two personal entities. The goal of *amar* is that another person might hear and understand and respond.[4]

Here in the opening verses of Holy Scripture we find the paradigm or model of community that weaves its way throughout the pages of holy writ. This vignette identifies the Holy Community for us. God the Father is speaking to the eternal Logos and directs him to create; in response to this *amar* of the Father, the eternal Logos goes forth and creates.

The Apostle John says of him:

> In the beginning was the Word (logos) and the Word was with God, and the Word was God. He was with God in the beginning. Through him all things were made; without him nothing was made that has been made. In him was life, and that life was the light of men. The light shines in the darkness, but the darkness has not understood it (John1:1–5; parenthetical insertion mine).

The Father spoke, giving the Son the necessary instructions, and the Son went forth to create whatever the Father willed. Note, as well, that this Holy Community of persons includes the Holy Spirit: "The Spirit of God was hovering over the waters" (Gen 1:2). In this passage of beginnings we have the biblical paradigm for relationships upon which human relationships should be modeled; distinct but equal persons laboring harmoniously together, as one, in a common cause to produce whatever they will.

ISRAEL: THE COMMUNITY OF GOD'S PEOPLE

There is an almost a plaintive cry issuing from God throughout the Old Testament record. God's deepest desire regarding Israel is that he wants them to be his own people.

---

4. Harris et al., *Theological Wordbook,* s.v. "amar"; see also Strong, *Exhaustive Concordance of the Bible* and Hebrew Dictionary.

The Adamic Covenant

As we view the Old Testament records of God's dealing with humanity we discover that he was continually endeavoring to establish for himself a people on the earth. First he created a man whom he named Adam, and from Adam's side he created the woman, whom Adam named Eve. God covenanted with the progenitors of our race, that is, he established the rules by which his relationship with this new humanity would be governed. Adam and Eve broke that covenant and rendered it null and void.

The Noahic Covenant

Next God endeavored to establish a community of his people through Noah and his children. This too failed when the sons of Noah violated the covenant made between their father and their God.

The Abramic Covenant

Following these failed attempts to gather to himself a people who would serve him out of love, God once again reached for a people for himself when he made a covenant with Abram. It was the Abramic covenant that ruled over the establishment of the nation of Israel as the community of God's people. This covenant established the rules by which the relationship between God and his people would be governed.

The Abramic covenant came to its fullness with the calling forth of God's people from Egypt and their being planted in the land of Palestine to become the nation of priests and kings God had foreordained. Israel as the community of God was intended to live together as his people in loving, caring, sharing, and ethically correct relationships. The covenant ruled over those relationships from both the Godward side and the Manward side. Israel did not keep the covenant, therefore, God declared the old covenant null and void and established a new covenant with a new people of God.

The Davidic Covenant

Jeremiah the prophet foretold the coming establishment of a new covenant and a new people of God:

> "The time is coming," declares the Lord, "when I will make a new covenant with the house of Israel and with the house of Judah. It will

not be like the covenant I made with their forefathers when I took them by the hand to lead them out of Egypt, because they broke my covenant, though I was a husband to them," declares the Lord.

"This is the covenant I will make with the house of Israel after that time," declares the Lord. "I will put my law in their minds and write it on their hearts. I will be their God, and they will be my people" (Jer 31:31–33).

The covenant Jeremiah foretold was the Davidic covenant, that covenant made between God and David, king of Israel. The heart of that covenant is found in 1 Chronicles 17:11–14:

I declare to you that the Lord will build a house for you: When your days are over and you go to be with your fathers, I will raise up your offspring to succeed you, one of your own sons, and I will establish his kingdom. He is the one who will build a house for me, and I will establish his throne forever. I will be his father, and he will be my son. I will never take my love away from him, as I took it away from your predecessor. I will set him over my house and my kingdom forever; his throne will be established forever.

This covenant has little to do with Solomon and the temple he built. This is the Davidic covenant that points to the coming of our Lord Jesus Christ. The son mentioned here is no other than Jesus. The house he will build is the new creation, the church, a new people of God governed by a new covenant that establishes the parameters of the relationship between God and this new people he has called to himself.

The Hebrew word for "house" in this passage is the word *bayith*, which is used primarily in the Old Testament to denote family.[5] God was not speaking of a temporal building of wood or stone; as Peter understood, he was speaking of living stones, the family of God's people, bound together in relationship with God and one another by this new covenant that Jesus purchased so that we who were not a people might become a people. Had God intended that we understand this house to be a temporal building, the Spirit would have chosen *birah*, or *hekhal*, or *miqdash*, or *mishkan*, all of which denote a temporal building of wood or stone. But he chose the word *bayith*, with its connotation of family and relationships and community.

---

5. Unger and White, *Expository Dictionary,* s.v. "bayith"; see also Strong, *Exhaustive Concordance* and Hebrew Dictionary.

THE NEW COMMUNITY OF GOD'S PEOPLE: THE CHURCH

The continuing paradigm or model we have just dealt with leads us directly to the New Testament, which is the new covenant with this new people of God. If the paradigm is consistent, we should expect that it would appear in the New Testament record. And, indeed, it does. It might surprise you as to where it is found, but it is there nonetheless. The paradigm is found in the gospel record where, on the Hebrew Feast of Unleavened Bread (Passover), Jesus observes this ancient feast with his disciples, whom he calls his *ecclesia,* or church (Matt 26:26–29). Passover is the celebration of the preservation, through covenant and obedience, of the Israelite families when the Death Angel passed through the land of Egypt, destroying the first born of any house that had not obeyed and placed the covering blood on the door posts of their home.

Calling Forth a People

It is not an accident that it is at this celebration, remembering the calling forth of the preserved families of the people of God out of Egypt, that Jesus institutes what we have come to call Communion, or the Lord's Supper. It is intentional; God planned it that way. For it is here that Jesus calls forth a new people of God to live in community together, under his lordship, governed by a new covenant that will set the parameters of their relationships and reign over them!

It is here that he foretells that, based upon his shed blood, this new covenant will provide the foundation for a new humanity—a new creation, a new Community of the people of God.

Indeed, the very elements of the Supper point with clarity to this new community. The vivid imagery portrayed by Jesus at that table was not lost on his disciples. They understood what he was saying to them. Not exhaustively, of course, but in seed form. They knew that they were at that moment celebrating the calling forth of a people, ancient Israel. They also may have surmised that Jesus was now calling for a new community, his church. W. D. Davies astutely observes that "the community gathered by Jesus was for Him the nucleus of a new Israel." Jesus's institution of the Eucharist was an "act of prophetic symbolism." "In the Eucharist," Davies continues, "the disciples are being treated as the nucleus of the 'New Israel.'"[6]

6. Davies, *Paul,* 101.

Paul acknowledges this imagery when dealing with the matter of the Lord's table in the Corinthian church. There he reminds them that observance of the Lord's Supper is no passive thing but something one actively participates in, not merely at the table, but at all times:

> Is not the cup of thanksgiving for which we give thanks a participation in the blood of Christ (new covenant)? And is not the bread we break a participation in the body of Christ (new community)? Because there is one loaf, we, who are many, are one body, for we all partake of the one loaf (1 Corinthians 10:16–17; parenthetical insertions mine).

The most ancient formula of the Lord's Supper available to us is that set down by Paul in 1 Corinthians 11. There Paul declares that the cup represents the new covenant that will govern the relationships of the new community of God, his body, the church.

We must understand the cup to point to the new covenant, for Paul explicitly states that is what it represents. In like manner we should understand the loaf to be that which Paul explicitly states it to be in chapter 10, representative of the church as the body of Christ, the new community.

Paul's use of the body to describe the church was not a device developed by him. He is merely taking up the imagery set forth by Jesus in designating this new community of faith to be his earthly body. That is what Jesus was calling forth on that Passover day. Even as they were celebrating the calling forth of ancient Israel, that people and the old covenant were being set aside for a new covenant and a new community of God's people.

That is what the church is all about. We are that new community. We are the people of God, called to live out the implications of the new covenant within the framework of the new community, demonstrating before the world that we can live together in ethically correct relationships under the grace of God. Relationships are primary with God![7]

A New Righteousness

It seems, however, that humanity is powerless to live righteously—that is, to live rightly related to one another. This is apparent in the church as much as it is in the world. God understood this dilemma of the human condition. A part of our salvation is the provision of his righteousness, which can enable us to function effectively under the ethical demands

---

7. Ibid., 108–10.

of the new covenant. The ethics of the kingdom are not merely an ideal, which, in our strength, we are to approximate. Jesus stated this caveat, "Without me you can do nothing" (John 15:5). He said this within the context of his teaching on fruit bearing. It should not surprise us that we do not live by the ethics of the kingdom, when we do not expect that the Holy Spirit will produce in us the fruit of that kingdom. We seem to be more concerned about charismatic matters than we are about the ethical manifestation of the Spirit in our lives.

John Drescher is correct in stating:

> Possession of any spiritual gift is never the only or even the primary evidence that a person has received the gift of the Holy Spirit. In the New Testament the primary evidence is not some charismatic, spectacular, or ecstatic gift or expression. The evidence of the Holy Spirit is moral and ethical. It is whether the life and spirit is Christlike. That is why the Apostle Paul says, "Anyone who does not have the Spirit of Christ does not belong to him" (Rom 8:9).[8]

True Spirit-filled living will be noted for its intentional demonstration of the character qualities of Jesus Christ in the believer's everyday living. The divine ability to live in right relationship with fellow believers, spouses, children, family members, and those outside the faith, exhibiting *agape* in those relationships, is the ultimate evidence of the Spirit-filled life. It does not matter if one can evidence what may appear to be all of the charismatic gifts of the Spirit; if the character of Jesus is not manifest in one's life, the validity of any charismata must come under question.

A SUGGESTED COMPREHENSIVE EVIDENTIAL CONSTRUCT

The task before us in this chapter is the formulation of a comprehensive evidential construct. I offer the following as a suggested alternative to existing evidential constructs in all Pentecostal bodies, to serve, at least, as a starting point for the rethinking of the relationship of glossolalia to Spirit-baptism.

In chapter 1 of this work it was demonstrated that the phenomenon of glossolalia was not unique to the experience of the disciples on the day of Pentecost. Rather, glossolalia had been practiced in the mystery religions for an extended period of time prior to the outpouring of the Holy Spirit

---

8. Drescher, *Spirit Fruit*, 23.

on the early church. It is acknowledged that the glossolalia in the mystery religions was certainly different from that produced by the Holy Spirit on the day of Pentecost in those first believers. Nevertheless, I posit here that since this is a fact of history that cannot be denied or ignored, the probability that glossolalia may be imitated by the demonic or mimicked by the flesh suggests that the use of speaking in tongues as the primary evidence that one has received the fullness of the Spirit is open to question.

This does not mean that the use of tongues as a first verifiable evidence, at the moment of Spirit-baptism, would be ruled out. Such a construct could stand if it were properly understood to mean that the Spirit truly is active in the life of the believer prior to and subsequent to this first verifiable evidence and that this evidence should not be construed to be primary and, thus, not necessarily inevitable. The subsequent growth of the believer in the grace and knowledge of Jesus Christ and the exhibited ethical manifestation of the Spirit in that person, through the concrete expression in everyday living of God's *agape,* must be considered as primary. This is the ultimate evidence that one is a Spirit-baptized, Spirit-filled, Spirit-led, child of God. It results in a life empowered by the Holy Spirit for holy living (ethical) and effective service (charismatic).

We have also seen in our look at patristic literature that there is no notion found there that glossolalia should be considered to be primary evidence of Spirit-baptism. On the contrary, though glossolalia was a contemporary phenomenon for many of the Fathers, we found explicit statements that the expression of *agape* should be considered as the evidence of being Spirit-filled. Clarke's observation of Basil's attitude toward glossolalia was cited: "He says that the Lord asked for love as the sign and test of discipleship, not signs and wonders, though He gives these in the Holy Ghost."[9] Also, Augustine affirms the notion that love is primary: "If then the witness of the presence of the Holy Ghost be not given through these miracles (glossolalia), what is it given . . . ? If he loves his brother, the Spirit of God dwelleth in him."[10]

These are explicit statements from historical theology affirming that *agape* was considered to be the ultimate evidence of Spirit-baptism in the post-apostolic church.

9. Clarke, *Works of Saint Basil,* 96.

10. Quoted in Hunter, "Tongues-Speech," 134 (parenthetical insertion mine).

The examination of Edward Irving and the Catholic Apostolic Church, the depository of the nineteenth-century Pentecostal revival, also affirms that *agape* must be considered as primary. To be sure, there was an inordinate emphasis on tongues by some of Irving's followers, but it has been demonstrated that the theologian, Irving, and those who followed him in leadership of the movement did not consider tongues as being the primary evidence of Spirit-baptism. We saw that Irving considered the ethical manifestation of the Spirit, in his sanctifying work, to be a prerequisite to the coming of the Spirit in fullness. As well, those who succeeded Irving in leadership of the movement looked not for glossolalic manifestations but for inward and outward manifestations of the Spirit's outpoured grace to serve as indicators of Spirit-baptism. They understood Spirit-baptism to be the believer's ordination into the universal priesthood of all believers and their empowerment for holy living and service.

An exploration of the biblical evidential paradigm revealed that Jesus established the paradigm both in the example of his life and death and in the explicit statement that his disciples would be identified by their manifestation of *agape*, God's love. Jesus's great concern for the ethical dimension of life surfaces throughout his teachings as recorded by the gospel evangelists, particularly in the Sermon on the Mount. Jesus said that the greatest love one can express is to lay down one's life for a friend. He went a step further than that when he laid down his life, not for friends, but for his enemies. For while we were yet enemies Christ died for us! Jesus said there can be no greater expression of love, anywhere! And, therefore, no greater evidence of the Spirit's presence in one's life.

Looking into Pauline theology, we discovered that Paul also considered *agape* to be the ultimate evidence of the Spirit-filled life. Possibly dealing with mistaken notions imported from the Greco/Roman mystery religions, from which the Corinthian converts undoubtedly came, he affirms that for pagans glossolalia may serve as a primary sign that one is possessed by their gods, but not so for Christians. In 1 Corinthians 13 we find his argument for the primary status of *agape* as the indicator or evidence of being filled with the Holy Spirit. In various other places in his writings Paul affirms the ultimate status of the ethical manifestations of the Spirit in the believer's life.

The bottom line in these considerations is that God's primary concern for his church and its interrelationships is not what believers do, rather, it is what they are. This can be stated in one word—*character*. If believers lack in character, that is, if ethical concerns are not addressed on a daily basis to result in righteous living, which in itself is the Spirit's expression of the character of Jesus in the believer, every charismatic manifestation denoted in the New Testament will not serve to verify that person is Spirit-baptized. The Holy Spirit will not deny his nature, nor will he contradict himself in either ethical or charismatic manifestation.

Rick Yohn reminds us:

> God has given two kinds of ability to the church. He has provided the potential for godly character which enables a believer to be. He has also distributed spiritual gifts which enable a believer to do. Both abilities are essential for the health of the Body, although being is more important than doing.[11]

Yohn reminds us further that "spiritual gifts are essential to serving the Lord in specific ministries. But spiritual character must control those gifts."[12] In noting the situation Paul dealt with at Corinth, Yohn observes that though the Corinthians were in Christ and indwelt by the Spirit, they had not progressed in maturity. Their spiritual gifts needed to be governed and enhanced by character, especially love. However, the manifestation of their spiritual gifts, rather than this loving character, had become the principal focus for their lives [13]

Character must be the first consideration in reconstructing an evidential concept. God in his self-disclosure has placed character as the primary factor in evidence that one is born of God. God is love. Those who are born of God love. Love is the greatest of God's gifts to the church. This love finds no greater expression than when one lays down one's life for one's friends. The world will know that we are his disciples as we love one another. Character can be stated in no finer terms than this.

The ultimate evidence of Spirit-baptism, then, can be said to occur in a believer's life when that person consistently manifests the ethical dimension of the new creation. This is evidencing the character of Jesus. It is the character of Jesus that Paul describes for us in his ode to love in 1 Corinthians 13. Love, insists Paul, is patient, kind, does not envy, does not boast, is not proud, is not rude, is not self-seeking, is not easily angered, keeps no record of wrongs, does not delight in evil, rejoices in truth, always protects, always

---

11. Yohn, *Spiritual Gifts,* 19.

12. Ibid., 22.

13. Ibid., 12.

trusts, always hopes, always perseveres, and never fails. This is how the Holy Spirit manifests the ethical dimension of the Christian life—the character of Jesus revealed in his people. Each of these manifestations has a direct bearing on the manner in which one person relates to another. This is what the Scriptures refer to as righteousness and holiness.

In conjunction with this ultimate evidence it is correct to affirm that expression of the charismata would be further evidence of the Spirit's presence This does not mean that any one charism of the Spirit would be given preference or elevated above the others. Rather, any of the charisms, in single manifestation or in combination, would serve as further evidence of the Spirit's fullness.

Should there be those who insist on focusing on glossolalia as a significant phenomenon related to Spirit-baptism, it is imperative that Wiebe's challenge to Pentecostals be acknowledged and dealt with,

> It seems to me that the most that defenders of Pentecostal views can claim concerning the relationship between glossolalia and Spirit baptism is that glossolalia is evidence (but not conclusive evidence) that Spirit baptism has occurred and that glossolalia, when it does occur, is probably caused by Spirit baptism. The view that glossolalia is the first effect of Spirit baptism receives no conclusive textual support. If that is what the initial evidence doctrine is taken to mean or at least imply, it is unfortunately indefensible.[14]

As noted in chapter 7, the most we can affirm regarding glossolalia and Spirit-baptism is that glossolalia could be viewed as the *first verifiable evidence* occurring at the time one is experiencing Spirit-baptism. Understood in this manner an initial evidence doctrine, if one must exist, might be palatable for many Christians.

The growth of the believer in the grace and knowledge of Jesus Christ and the ethical manifestation of God's love exhibited in everyday living must be considered primary. This is the ultimate evidence that one is a Spirit-baptized, Spirit-filled, Spirit-led child of God. It should result in a life empowered by the Holy Spirit for holy living (ethical) and effective service (charismatic). "All men will know that you are my disciples, if you love one another" (John 13:35).

---

14. Wiebe, "Initial Evidence," 472.

Appendix

Do All Speak with Tongues?

An open letter to ministers and saints
of the Pentecostal movement

F. F. Bosworth

A WONDERFUL REVIVAL

THE PAST FEW YEARS have witnessed one of the most wonderful and far reaching revivals of the Christian era—a revival of power, one to which God has borne witness "with signs and wonders, and divers miracles, and gifts of the Holy Ghost." Many thousands have spoken in supernatural tongues as on the Day of Pentecost, as a result of the same mighty Baptism that came upon that waiting company in the upper room. The multitude blessed by this world-wide visitation comprises men of all walks of life from the most illiterate to men of the highest scholarship, including many leaders in spiritual thought, and from the poorest to the richest and affluent. Thousands have been healed through "the prayer of faith," James 5:14–15 of all manner of diseases and afflictions. We have witnessed many scores of miraculous healings as definite and wonderful as any recorded in the New Testament. Not only the manifestation of tongues and healing, but all the other signs that accompanied the first outpouring of the Spirit have been more or less in evidence. Not merely instances here and there, which all Christians know have occurred at different intervals, but thousands of cases all over the world, until I think we are safe in saying there has been more preaching and writing on these matters, both for and against, than at any period of church history. And it is proper that there should be, because it is all important that we ascertain the truth upon this great subject of spiritual manifestations. Paul said, "It is important, brethren, that you should have clear knowledge on the subject of spiritual gifts." (Weymouth's translation) 1 Cor. 12:1.

Certainly in these days of waning spirituality among the masses of professors, and the uncertainty everywhere manifested, there is no greater need than that every believer be brought under the full sway of the Spirit of God, each one not only having the Spirit, but also "the manifestation of the Spirit," which "is given to every man to profit withal. 1 Cor. 12:7. Anything short of this limits the Holy Spirit and mars God's gracious plan for each life. In this Laodicean period of the Church age, when, so many professors are "lovers of pleasures more than lovers of God," not only without the power, but even "denying the power," 2 Tim. 3:5, the crying need is for instruction that will inspire faith and bring the Church back to her ancient moorings where every member of the body of Christ will again realize that the work of God is accomplished, "not by might, nor by power, (of ours), but by the Spirit of the Lord." Zech. 4:6. It is a deplorable fact that in many modern churches and revivals the manifestations of Spirit are never thought of, but, more dependence is placed in the wisdom of which the Bible says is fool-ishness, 1 Cor. 3:19. How few ministers and evangelists today can say, "Our gospel came not to you in word only, but also in power, in the Holy Ghost, and in much assurance." 1 Thes.1:5. Or, "My speech and my preaching was not with enticing words of man's wisdom, but in demonstration of the Spirit and of power, that your faith should not stand in the wisdom of men, but in the power of God." 1 Cor. 2:5–6.

In this gracious revival or movement, there developed two elements which we might call Conservatives and Radicals, or Extremists. And the outside world have received impressions from one or the other of two factions. Where the conservative has been followed, there has been a breaking down of prejudice, and the steady triumph of truth along the lines of spiritual manifestations. Hearts and minds have been enlightened, which always creates deep hunger and abandonment to the Spirit's operation. Thus God has been able to manifest it to and through the saints in divers ways for the common good. The clearly defined truth concerning Divine Healing is now making its way into pulpits formerly silent on this subject, and the people are being frankly told that "the prayer of faith shall save the sick." James 5:14–15. And many other New Testament truths are being revived and preached with no uncertain sound. Thank God for every voice lifted in defense of the simple, powerful, primitive Gospel.

On the other hand, where radicalism has prevailed the result has been, and always will be, disastrous to the cause of religion, resulting in strife, anarchy, wild and unreasonable extremes, and hard, harsh, critical, censorious spirits, so unlike the meek and lowly Christ. Instead of having "form without power," they have "noise without power." These conditions have been the cause of deep-seated prejudice in the minds of many good people who have been stumbled and held back because of these inconsistencies and fanatical tendencies among the professors of these wonderful experiences.

A DOCTRINAL ERROR

Error in teaching is another cause of trouble, and is mainly responsible for so much of the superficial work and consequent irregularities, which Satan has used to turn aside thousands of hungry souls. The purpose of this letter is to point out what I consider a serious doctrinal error, the elimination of which will solve many of our difficulties, besides opening the way for more of the manifestations of the Spirit, and a much deeper work of God. The error to which I refer is the doctrine held by many, that the Baptism in the Spirit is in every instance evidenced by the initial physical sign of speaking in other tongues as the Spirit gives utterance, Acts 2:4, and that this is not the gift of tongues, referred to in Paul to the Corinthians. 1 Cor. 12.

WAS THE SPEAKING IN TONGUES AT PENTECOST THE GIFT OF TONGUES?

After eleven years in the work on Pentecostal lines (during which time it has been my privilege to see thousands receive the precious Baptism in the Holy Spirit), I am certain that those who receive the most powerful Baptisms for service do not receive the manifestation of speaking in tongues. And I am just as certain many who seemingly speak in tongues, are not nor ever have been Baptized in the Spirit. Although I have in the past very tenaciously contended for it, as many of the brethren still do, I am certain that it is entirely wrong and unscriptural to teach that the miraculous speaking in tongues on the Day of Pentecost was not the gift of tongues God set in the Church, and which is so often mentioned in the first letter to the Corinthians. Not only is there not a solitary passage of Scripture on which to base this doctrine, but on the other hand the Scriptures flatly deny it. That there is no Scripture for this "distinction," speaking in tongues as the Spirit gave utterance at Jerusalem, and the gift of tongues at Corinth, is being seen and admitted by Bible students and teachers in the Pentecostal movement. In fact, some in the movement have never believed this distinction was Scriptural.

At a recent State Council of the Assemblies, when the Chairman of the Council was asked by one of the young ministers if there was a passage or a number of passages on which to base this distinction, he publicly admitted that there was not a single passage. Charles F. Parham, who came forward with this doctrine in the year 1900, was the first man in the history of the world, publicly to teach this doctrine. He saw that it was not possible to teach that speaking in tongues will in every case accompany the Baptism in the Spirit, unless he could make it appear that the speaking in tongues on the day of Pentecost was something distinct from the gift of tongues at Corinth. He was first to teach that none have been Baptized in the Spirit except those who have spoken in tongues. The fact is that hundreds of the greatest soul winners of the entire Christian era, without the gift of tongues, have had a much greater enduement of power and have been used to accomplish a much greater and deeper work than has Mr. Parham.

The argument that the miraculous manifestation of tongues on the Day of Pentecost is distinct from the gift of tongues, called in the Scriptures "the manifestation of the Spirit," falls flat when we consider the 7th and 8th verses of the 12th chapter of 1 Corinthians. In the 7th verse Paul says, "The manifestation of the Spirit is given to every man to profit withal." Some have taught and written that "the manifestation of the Spirit" here mentioned is always the speaking in tongues as the Spirit gives utterance on the Day of Pentecost. They claim that is for all who receive the Baptism in the Spirit, but that it is not the gift of tongues mentioned in the same chapter. But in the next verse Paul entirely demolishes this argument by explaining what "the manifestation of the Spirit" is. "For to one," he says, "is given by the Spirit the word of Wisdom; to answer the word of knowledge the same Spirit; to another faith by the same Spirit; to another the gifts of healing by the same Spirit; to another the working of miracles; to another prophecy; to another discerning of spirits; to another divers kinds of tongues; to another the interpretation of tongues; but all these worketh that one and the selfsame Spirit, dividing to every man severally as He will." Each one of these nine gifts is called the manifestation of the Spirit. God's definition of a gift is "the manifestation of the Spirit." The speaking in tongues on the day of Pentecost was "the manifestation of the Spirit," and therefore is identical with the gift of tongues, about which Paul writes to the Corinthians. These Galileans had no power in themselves, without the Spirit, to speak in these languages, but it was given them by the Spirit to utter words and form sentences not originating in their own minds. We therefore contend that this was the gift of tongues that God set in the Church.

The fact here mentioned that the gift of tongues is always "the manifestation of the Spirit," refutes the theory held by many that the gift of tongues is the ability to speak in tongues at will. The word of God discountenances all speaking in tongues except that which is "the manifestation of the Spirit." The eleventh verse makes this clear by saying that the Spirit works each of these manifestations or as Weymouth translates it, "These results are all brought about by the Spirit." In other words, the Holy Spirit uses us instead of our using Him. God, we are told in this chapter, has set these gifts or manifestations in the Church. If the speaking in tongues on the day of Pentecost was not the gift of tongues, I ask you when did God set the gift of tongues in the church? Chapter and verse please. The Scriptures tell us that when Christ ascended up on high He gave gifts unto men. Eph. 4:8–12.

Another argument used in the attempt to prove that the gift of tongues is not speaking as the Spirit gives utterance is based upon Paul's instructions to those with the gift of tongues to be silent in the church, unless there is an interpreter. They argue that if Paul told them to keep silent, it is proof that it was not the Spirit's utterance, because that would be rebuking the Holy Ghost. This idea arises from the mistaken notion that the manifestation of the Spirit in tongues is always for the public, whereas Paul said, "If there be no interpreter (present) let him keep silence in the church, and let him speak to himself and to God."

It is a great mistake to think that the manifestation of tongues must always be spoken to the church, and that it will be quenching the Spirit to obey Paul's inspired instruction to speak "unto himself and to God." Ignorance here has made much confusion in Pentecostal assemblies. Many after disobeying these inspired directions say, "I could not help it." This is a mistake, for Paul commands silence unless there is an interpreter. Sometimes, when the church is being greatly edified by a sermon, there may be many at the same time who feel like worshiping God in tongues, but this may be controlled without quenching the Spirit, for Paul says that even where there is an interpreter only one should speak at a time. Even the greater manifestation of prophecy, which is especially for the edification of the Church, is to be restrained, so that the prophets shall speak "one by one that all may learn, and all may be comforted." The Apostle evidently purposed effectually to cure the Corinthians of the can't help it idea, that caused so much confusion in the Corinthian church, and is doing the same thing in these days. He tells them distinctly that God is not the author of this confusion, but that "the spirits of the prophets are subject to the prophets." Of course we are always glad when God, in the middle of our sermon, saves and baptizes souls, and gives them the speaking in tongues, as He did while Peter preached to the household of Cornelius.

THE DOCTRINE NEVER MENTIONED IN ANY EPISTLE

But once again as to the supposed distinction between tongues in the Acts and at Corinth, after which we will leave you to an impartial searching of the Scriptures touching this point.

It is insisted that the speaking in tongues in the Acts was temporary, and that every Christian should speak in tongues as the initial sign of being Baptized in the Spirit; while the gift of tongues dealt with in Paul's letter to the Corinthians implies permanence, and that few have the permanent gift. If this theory is correct, with its necessary distinction between tongues and tongues, then we agree that it is the most important doctrine of the New Testament, for what can be more important than for Christians to receive the enduement of power so necessary to accomplish the work that God wants done? Then is it not strange that not one of the inspired writers of any of the epistles to the New Testament Churches, preachers and saints scattered abroad, ever made the slightest reference to that kind of speaking in tongues which, as many allege, is the evidence of the Baptism? Think of it, and then think again, all the New Testament epistles and not a single mention of this doctrine. We hear in these letters of backsliding from almost every other doctrine, even the truth of justification by faith, the resurrection from the dead, and the second coming of Christ. They backslid from the great truths of faith and love, and the apostles were careful to line them up and get them straight, but if they ever held the doctrine of "tongues as the evidence," they never once deviated from it, but held it so tenaciously that not even a word of exhortation was deemed necessary to keep them from letting down on this point. Will any of the brethren make the charge that the writers of these epistles had compromised on the question of the Baptism in the Spirit before writing all of these letters?

The doctrine that all are to speak in tongues when Baptized in the Spirit is based entirely upon supposition without a solitary "Thus saith the Lord." It is nowhere taught in the Scriptures, but is assumed from the fact that in three instances recorded in the Acts they spoke in tongues as a result of the Baptism. While this notable fact should serve as an eye-opener to those who contend against any speaking in tongues, it is by no means a conclusive proof that God gave the same gift to all the multiplied thousands added to the church during this most marvelous period of church history extending over more than a quarter of a century.

God always has a definite purpose and an infinitely wise reason for everything He does. The Day of Pentecost witnessed the grandest and most effective display of the gift of tongues the world has ever seen. And God's purpose was that it should be "a sign," not to believers, but to the unbelieving Jews dwelling at Jerusalem "out of every nation under heaven." And God's purpose was most wonderfully realized, for three thousand unbelieving Jews were, by the fact that these Galileans spoke in their own languages, forced to believe that Jesus was actually the Messiah. Perhaps there was no other sign that God could have manifested so effectively under these circumstances as the speaking in tongues. Eight years later Peter and the six Jewish brethren who accompanied him to the household of Cornelius were, with all other Jews, unbelievers all to the Gentiles being included in the privileges of the gospel. So God made the gift of tongues a sign to them, thus convincing them, to their astonishment, that "God also to the Gentiles hath granted repentance unto life." When Peter returned to Jerusalem, the apostles and brethren contended with him, saying, "Thou wentest in to men uncircumcised, and didst eat with them." So Peter rehearsed the matter from the beginning and closed his argument by saying, "As I began to speak, the Holy Ghost fell on them, as on us at the beginning." If the thousands who were saved during that wonderful revival period of eight years between the second and the tenth chapters of Acts, spoke in tongues when Baptized in the Spirit, why did Peter say, "as on us at the beginning"? He could just as well have said, "As He has been baptizing all from the beginning." If it was well known that all these spoke in tongues when they were Baptized in the Spirit, why should he point back only to the time when they spoke in tongues on the Day of Pentecost? Again, years later, when Paul met the brethren at Ephesus who had never heard that there was any Holy Ghost, God gave them both tongues and prophecy when they received the Spirit. And if Luke was so careful to record it when only these few spoke in tongues, why did he not record it when all the many thousands since Pentecost spoke in tongues, if they all did?

If it be objected here that perhaps the multitudes added to the church during this unparalleled revival period did not receive the Holy Ghost, let it be remembered that in apostolic days converts were not left in the dark concerning the Baptism in the Spirit as they are in modern revivals. Peter declared to the multitude on the Day of Pentecost that as many as would repent would receive the gift of the Holy Ghost; that the promise was unto them and to their children, etc., Acts 2:38–39. And it is distinctly stated of the three thousand added "to the church on that day," that "they all continued steadfastly in the apostles' doctrine and fellowship," proving that they all received the Holy Ghost. The Baptism in the Holy Spirit held an important place in the apostles' doctrine and is clearly stated in Peter's first sermon. We read in the eighth chapter of Acts that as soon as the apostles at Jerusalem had heard about the revival at Samaria they sent unto them Peter and John, who prayed for them that they might receive the Holy Ghost. And when Paul met the brethren at Ephesus, his first question was, "Have ye received the Holy Ghost since ye believed?" By reading the epistles, we find that all the churches had received the Baptism in the Spirit.

Another argument used in the attempt to prove that all spirit-baptized believers will speak in tongues is based upon John 15:26–27: "When the Comforter is come . . . He shall testify of Me and ye shall bear witness." It is contended that because two testimonies are here spoken of, one is the Holy Ghost speaking in tongues. But in Heb. 2:4 we are told how the Holy Ghost testifies, or bears witness. "God also bearing them witness, both with signs and wonders, and with divers miracles, and gifts (not the gift of tongues only) of the Holy Ghost according to His own will."

The fact is that it is unscriptural to teach that they received that one manifestation, and this is the force of all of Paul's argument to the Corinthians. For instance, from the 12th verse to the close of the 14th chapter Paul teaches the exact opposite of what many today are teaching, endeavoring to show them that all are not to expect the same manifestation of the Spirit. He uses the illustration of the human body and its members and asks, "If the whole body were an eye, where were the hearing?" etc., and then, to make it still more emphatic, he asks, "I ask are all apostles? are all prophets? are all teachers? are all workers of miracles? have all the gifts of healing ? do all speak with tongues? do all interpret?" Of course the answer to each of these questions is No. In other words, Paul is distinctly saying that all are not teachers, and all do not speak in tongues.

We can't dodge this question by saying that this is the gift of tongues and not the speaking in tongues as on the Day of Pentecost, because, as already shown, Paul distinctly states that this is "the manifestation of the Spirit," making it identical with the manifestation of the Spirit that came on the Day of Pentecost.

GIFTS NOT FOR EVIDENCE BUT FOR SERVICE

Teaching that tongues is the evidence of the Baptism in the Spirit makes it a sign to believers, whereas Paul distinctly says that it is not a sign to the believer, but to the unbeliever. If made a sign to the seeker for the Baptism, it not only leaves no place for faith, but on the other hand destroys faith already Divinely given. After God has most powerfully Baptized the seeker, and, with perfect faith Divinely inwrought, he is rejoicing with joy unspeakable and full of glory, with every ounce of his flesh quivering under the power of the indwelling Spirit, some one will tell him that he has not yet received the Holy Ghost because he did not speak in tongues. This destroys his faith, which Paul says is both "the evidence" and "the substance," Heb. 11:1, and sends him home discouraged, to continue his seeking, as some have for several years. Everywhere I have gone I have met hungry souls who seemingly speak in tongues, but who have not this assuring faith that they are Baptized in the Spirit. Nothing short of real faith can satisfy the heart and put the soul at rest. The word "evidence" in the Scriptures is never used in connection with a spiritual gift, or manifestation, making faith to depend upon any sign or physical manifestation, but the Apostle distinctly states that "faith is the evidence." Anything that is to be received in answer to prayer is to be received by faith, even the great miracle of the new birth, and Paul expressly states that we are to "receive the promise of the Spirit through faith," Gal. 3:14. Nothing short of faith can satisfy the heart and give us power. Paul said, "Let everything be done with a view to building up faith," but the "tongues evidence" teaching reverses this, not only destroying faith, but making it impossible until the gift of tongues is received. This teaching causes people to reject the mightiest Baptism in the Spirit, disregarding the personal Holy Spirit within, and puts them from that time on seeking for years, in many instances, for a physical manifestation, that Paul plainly teaches us all are not to expect, for the Spirit is to divide the manifestations "as He will."

This teaching, besides destroying faith, puts some to seeking a hundred times after God has Baptized them in the Spirit, in many instances much more powerfully than others who spoke in tongues. It is absurd to suppose that Jesus must pour out the Spirit upon the same persons a hundred times before He succeeds in getting them Baptized in the Spirit. There is not a single instance like this in the Scriptures. John the Baptist completed the work the first time he undertook to baptize those who came to him. And so with Jesus, according to the Scriptures. He never had to make two attempts to administer His Baptism. Jesus taught that the first time the Spirit comes upon a consecrated seeker He is to "abide forever." And I insist that when a consecrated seeker has been correctly instructed, he should receive the Holy Ghost the first time the Spirit falls upon him.

Again, this telling those who have been Baptized in the Spirit that they have not been so Baptized because they did not get the gift of tongues also robs them of a testimony for months and even years, and puts them to seeking for a physical manifestation when they ought to be witnessing and laboring for souls. Jesus said, "Ye shall receive the power of the Holy Ghost coming upon you; and ye shall be My witnesses." Acts 1:8 R.V.

If allowed to believe, their testimony under the power of the Spirit would have led others into the Baptism. Instead of this those who might have been led into the Baptism by their testimony, have watched them seek for hours after the Holy Spirit had fallen upon them, and this has discouraged many, delaying the revival that much, besides denying Christ's encouraging words, "How much more shall your heavenly Father give the Holy Ghost to them that ask Him?" Luke 11:13.

It is a notable fact that many of the deepest and best teachers and preachers in the Pentecostal movement have the poorest success in getting the seekers through to speaking in tongues. The reason is they are too conscientious to use the "Glory-glory-glory-say-it-a-little-faster" and other similar methods, which have made some of the shallowest and most fanatical workers apparently the most successful. Proper instruction followed by consecration and prayer will, in every instance, bring down the Baptism in the Holy Spirit, but it will not always bring down the manifestation of tongues. Repeated seeking and methods never used in the Scriptures have been employed to get all the seekers through to the "Bible evidence," so called, and then I am certain that many who have the Baptism and seemingly speak in tongues, do not really do so, although they are sincere in the matter. This over-emphasis in teaching tongues and the employment of unscriptural methods is responsible for this. I recently heard a prominent minister in the Pentecostal movement preaching from the tenth chapter of Acts. For nearly an hour he insisted that unless we press the "tongues evidence" teaching the people will not receive the Holy Ghost. He overlooked the fact that Peter, in this chapter, had better success in getting his audience through to the Baptism without even mentioning the subject, than any preacher in modern times has had by preaching that tongues is the Bible evidence. While Peter was preaching to them, about Jesus, they all received the Baptism, to the astonishment of Peter himself. I am determined never to try to get any seeker to speak in tongues until after I see God tries to get them to do so, but then if they are not yielding or cooperating properly, I will instruct them to yield to and "obey the Spirit." This will leave the proper place for faith, and I have found that it will bring the real speaking in tongues much quicker, for where any sign is placed before faith, it hinders the Spirit, and lessens the power. Jesus taught that "these signs shall follow" faith, and not "faith shall follow these signs."

NO "THUS SAITH THE LORD"

We have no "Thus saith the Lord" in the Scriptures that all are to speak in tongues, but the very opposite, as shown, but we have many a "Thus saith the Lord" as to other Bible evidences, or rather results of the Baptism in the Spirit. For instance: "They all prophecy," "He will convict the world of sin," "He will guide you into all truth," "He will take the things of Mine and show them unto you," "He will glorify Me," "Ye shall receive the power of the Holy Ghost coming upon you," "He will make intercessions through the saints with groanings that cannot be uttered," "Ye shall be endued with power from on high," etc.

The Scriptures tell us that Jesus is the Author and the Finisher of our faith, Heb.12:2, and He never taught this doctrine that all Spirit-baptized believers would speak in tongues. Then why should we? Not one apostle or prophet, and not one of the world's great soul winners ever taught it. So it is clear that this doctrine is not essential to the greatest success. On the other hand, it greatly circumscribes our usefulness by shutting out those who are so well versed in the Scriptures that we can not convince them of our unscriptural theory. It will split any church wide open, separating equally devout Christians, unless we can make them all believe it. Even those who speak in tongues, equally devout among the Pentecostal ministry, cannot agree on this point. For God does not want them to agree upon a theory for which there is not a solitary passage of Scripture, making it a test of fellowship and a basis upon which to build a new church. When we, as a movement, will confine ourselves to what the Scriptures plainly teach upon this important subject of the Baptism and all the manifestations of the Spirit, and preach the great things about the Baptism in the Holy Ghost, our usefulness will be enhanced manifold.

VALUE OF TONGUES AND PROPHESY COMPARED

In 1 Cor. 14:1, we see that these Spirit-baptized church members, some of whom did not speak in tongues, were instructed to "be eager in their pursuit of love, and to be earnestly ambitious for spiritual gifts," but chiefly that they might prophesy, which Paul says is speaking "unto men to edification and exhortation and comfort" as a "manifestation of the Spirit." In most of our meetings seekers are not so instructed. The teaching on tongues as the evidence makes them more ambitious to speak in tongues than to prophesy. Prophecy, which Joel said would be the most prominent result of the Baptism in the Spirit, Joel 2:28, and which Paul taught was the most valuable "manifestation of the Spirit," is not sought in many Pentecostal meetings nor even recognized as an evidence of the Baptism where it is already manifested.

In the fourth verse, Paul contrasts the value of these two manifestations by saying, "He that speaketh in tongues edifieth himself but he that prophesieth edifieth the church."

Why not consider the more valuable "manifestation of the Spirit" as at least as good an evidence that One is Baptized in the Spirit as the less valuable manifestation? Joel said that when the Spirit was poured out they would prophesy, and certainly this means that they could not do it before. In the fifth verse Paul says, "I should be right glad were you all to speak in tongues (proving they did not all speak), but yet more glad were you all to prophesy." (Weymouth) This is not the way we have felt about it in some of our meetings. Why not? Why not feel like Paul did in this matter? Surely he had not compromised and let down as some are charged with doing as soon as they teach as Paul did. In the same verse Paul gives his reason for being more glad when they prophesy. "In fact," he says, "the man who prophesies is superior to him who speaks in tongues, except when the latter interprets in order that the church may get a blessing." (Weymouth) Why should we say that the man who is superior and has the more valuable "manifestation of the Spirit" is not Baptized in the Spirit, and the inferior man is, because he has a "manifestation of the Spirit" less in value? This verse also proves that some prophesied who did not speak in tongues. We read in Acts 18:11 that Paul preached eighteen months to the Corinthians, but did not get them all to speak in tongues.

Then why should we expect to get all to speak in tongues? I have known some to receive the gift of interpretation when they were Baptized in the Spirit who did not receive the gift of tongues. And this is Scriptural, for Paul writes, "to one divers kinds of tongues; to another the interpretation of tongues."

In the 12th verse we are instructed to be ambitious for the manifestations of the Spirit most edifying to the church, and therefore for those who speak in tongues to pray for the power to interpret. In the 18th verse Paul thanks God that he spoke in tongues more than they all, "But in the church," he says, "I had rather speak five words with my understanding, that by my voice I might teach others also, than ten thousand words in an unknown tongue." He then tells them not to be children in understanding, implying that it is childish for all to prefer the spiritual manifestation of less value to the church. Paul concludes this subject by telling them to be "earnestly ambitious to prophesy, and not to check speaking in tongues."

Let it not be supposed that I am depreciating God's glorious gift of tongues because I do not believe that this one manifestation always accompanies the Baptism in the Spirit. God graciously gave me this gift fourteen years ago, and nearly every day in prayer and worship I still speak in tongues, and it is one of the sweetest things in my Christian experience. In every revival I am privileged to conduct, God graciously bestows upon many the gift of tongues, for which I always praise Him, but for several years I have never told the people that this is the one necessary evidence of the Baptism, but that it is just one of the manifestations of the Spirit that results from the Baptism. I find that the people get deeper into God and have more power when they are not taught in such a way that they anchor in tongues; and that the work is much easier and deeper where seekers are allowed to believe when God pours the Spirit upon them. I have been convicted over the shallowness and instability of many of the converts who profess the Baptism under the 'tongues evidence' teaching. Every place I have gone to help Pentecostal Assemblies in revivals some have come to me and said, "Brother Bosworth, pray for me, I have spoken in tongues, but I am not satisfied."

THE GREATEST PHASE OF THE BAPTISM

I am determined that those converted in my meetings shall expect and receive a real Baptism of Power that will put them under the sway of the Spirit and in loving sympathy with Christ in His great work of saving a lost world. To me the greatest phase of the Baptism in the Spirit is the spontaneous life of intercession. Paul said the Spirit Himself would make intercession through the saint with groanings that cannot be uttered, Rom. 8:26, and I have seen Spirit-baptized souls, some with and others without the manifestation of tongues, carried clear out and beyond themselves into the ever-flowing stream of Christ's intercessions for a lost world, experiencing that exquisite love that enabled them to "offer up prayers and supplications with strong crying and tears," Heb. 5:7; until they were heard. I believe there is no other "manifestation of the Spirit" that means so much to God, to the church, and to a lost world, for it is in this intercession that both the Christian and the church are to find and wield their highest power. In this way each Christian, as the Prophet Isaiah said, can "make his voice to be heard on high, to loose the bands of wickedness, to undo the heavy burdens, and to let the oppressed go free." Isa. 58:6–8. One name of the Holy Ghost is "The Spirit of Grace and Supplications," Zech. 12:10, and one of the great marks of the Baptism in the Spirit is a power in prayer hitherto unknown. In this phase of the Baptism there are possibilities whose limits never have been found, It was this power working in Spirit-baptized saints at Rochester, N. Y., under the ministry of Charles G. Finney, that brought about eighty thousand conversions in six months. Finney, himself, said: "I would not give my Spirit of prayer for the intellectual endowments of an Archangel." One man in Finney's day, while on a sick bed dying with tuberculosis, noted in his little memorandum book the dates when he was enabled to pray the prayer of faith for revivals in thirty different localities. After the man died God poured His Spirit in a gracious revival upon each of these places. I have seen many who were the deepest in intercession and soul travail who have never spoken in tongues, and among those who professed the Baptism in the Spirit under the "tongues evidence" teaching I have met hundreds who have not been full enough of the Spirit to be carried out of themselves into the intercessions of Christ. It is said of the three thousand converted on the Day of Pentecost that "they all continued steadfastly . . . in prayer." Surely, those who have the greatest love and compassion for souls and the greatest Spirit of prayer have the most of the Holy Ghost, whether they speak in tongues or not. I have told the young converts every place I have been that unless they got a Baptism that gave them the Spirit of prayer, I would consider my ministry, as far as they were concerned, a failure. We have a positive "Thus saith the Lord" that the Spirit will make intercessions through the saints, and if this had been preached as "The Bible Evidence of the Baptism," the work as a whole would be deeper.

Teaching the people that speaking in tongues, is to be the evidence to them that they are Baptized in the Spirit stands in the way of faith, destroys faith already Divinely given, robs the Baptized believer of a testimony until he receives the manifestation of tongues, puts him again, although already baptized, to seeking for a physical manifestation perhaps less in value than the one already received; wears out the workers at the altar by praying for weeks and even months for those upon whom the Lord has poured His Spirit many times; delays the revival just that much; discourages others from seeking and denies Christ's encouraging words, "How much more shall your Heavenly Father give the Holy Ghost to them that ask Him?" Luke 11:13. I find that by standing right with the Scriptures, with regard to all these manifestations of the Spirit, our revivals will be deeper and quicker, and we will be free from many of the irregularities and much of the fanaticism that has torn up the work and hurt the cause of God in so many localities. I have been waiting for some of the other Pentecostal brethren to come out with literature on this line, but I guess they have been a little timid, like myself, so I have felt it my plain duty to my brethren to write this for their perusal. I know I will lose the friendship of some who may not be able to see the truth herein contained, but if I can be a help to others, opening the way for their greater usefulness, I will feel well repaid. I am sure if our movement could be free from this one error in teaching, and would preach the greater things about the Baptism, our opportunities for usefulness would be increased manyfold. The way would then be opened for more of the manifestations or gifts of the Spirit, and consequently the revivals would be greater and deeper.

May God speed this day is my prayer;
F. F. BOSWORTH
(n.d.)

Bibliography

Aker, Ben C. "Some Reflections on Pentecostal Hermeneutics." *Paraclete*, Spring 1985, 18–20.

Anderson, Ray S. *Theological Foundations for Ministry*. Grand Rapids: Wm. B. Eerdmans Publishing Co., 1979.

Anderson, Robert M. *Vision of the Disinherited*. New York: Oxford University Press, 1979.

Atter, Gordon F. *The Third Force*. Peterborough, Ont.: College Press, 1970.

Bach, Marcus. *The Inner Ecstasy*. New York: World Publishing Co., 1969.

Bainton, Roland H. *Christendom*. 2 vols. New York: Harper & Row, 1966.

Barclay, Oliver R. *The Intellect and Beyond*. Grand Rapids: Academie Books, Zondervan, 1985.

Barclay, William. *Flesh and Spirit*. Grand Rapids: Baker Book House, 1976.

———. *The Letters to the Corinthians*. Philadelphia: Westminster Press, 1975.

———. *The Old Law & the New Law*. Philadelphia: Westminster Press, 1972.

———. *The Promise of the Spirit*. Philadelphia: Westminster Press, 1976.

Barnette, Henlee H. *Introducing Christian Ethics*. Nashville: Broadman Press, 1961.

Barney, Kenneth D. *The Fellowship of the Holy Spirit*. Springfield, MO: Gospel Publishing House, 1977.

Barnstone, Willis. *The Other Bible*. San Francisco: Harper & Row, 1984.

Barratt, T. B. *In the Days of the Latter Rain*. London: Elim Publishing Co., 1928.

Barth, Karl. *The Christian Life*. Grand Rapids: Wm. B. Eerdmans Publishing Co., 1981.

———. *Church Dogmatics A Selection*. San Francisco: Harper & Row, 1962.

———. *The Doctrine of the Word of God*. Edinburgh: T. & T. Clark, 1955.

———. *The Humanity of God*. Richmond: John Knox Press, 1972.

Bartleman, Frank. *Another Wave of Revival*. Springdale, PA: Whitaker House, 1982.

———. *How Pentecost Came to Los Angeles: As It Was in the Beginning, Old Azusa mission— From My Diary*. Los Angeles: F. Bartleman, 1925.

Basham, Don W. *A Handbook on Tongues, Interpretation and Prophecy*. Monroeville, PA: Whitaker Books, 1971.

———. *Ministering the Baptism in the Holy Spirit*. Monroeville, PA: Whitaker Books, 1971.

———. *The Miracle of Tongues*. Old Tappan, NJ: Fleming H. Revell Co., 1973.

Bassett, William, and Peter Huizing, eds. *Experience of the Spirit*. Concilium. New York: Seabury Press, 1974–76.

Baus, Karl. *From the Apostolic Community to Constantine*. Edited by Hubert Jedin and John Patrick Dolan. Vol. 1, *History of the Church*, edited by Hubert Jedin and John Patrick Dolan. New York: Seabury Press, Crossroad, 1980.

Beardslee, William. *A Literary Criticism of the New Testament*. Philadelphia: Fortress Press, 1970.

Bennett, Dennis J. *The Holy Spirit and You.* Plainfield, NJ: Logos International, 1971.

———. *Nine O'clock in the Morning.* Plainfield, NJ: Logos International, 1970.

Bergsma, Stuart. *Speaking with Tongues.* Grand Rapids: Baker Book House, 1965.

Berkhof, Louis. *Principles of Biblical Interpretation.* Grand Rapids: Baker Book House, 1950.

Berkouwer, G. C. *General Revelation.* Grand Rapids: Wm. B. Eerdmans Publishing Co., 1955.

Bicket, Zenas J. *Walking in the Spirit.* Springfield, MO: Gospel Publishing House, 1977.

Bivin, David, and Roy Blizzard, Jr. *Understanding the Difficult Words of Jesus.* Austin, TX: Center for Judaic-Christian Studies, 1984.

Bloch-Hoell, Nils. *The Pentecostal Movement.* New York: Humanities Press, 1964.

Bloesch, Donald G. *Christian Foundations.* 7 vols. Downers Grove, IL: InterVarsity Press, 1992–2004.

———. *Essentials of Evangelical Theology.* 2 vols. San Francisco: Harper & Row, 1978.

———. *The Reform of the Church.* Eugene, OR: Wipf and Stock, 1998.

———. *Wellsprings of Renewal.* Grand Rapids: Wm. B. Eerdmans Publishing Co., 1974.

Blumhofer, Edith Waldvogel. *The Assemblies of God: A Popular History.* Springfield, MO: Radiant Books, Gospel Publishing House, 1985.

Blumhofer, Edith. "The Great Oneness—Trinitarian Debate." *Heritage,* Fall 1985, 6–8.

Boice, James M. *Foundations of the Christian Faith.* Vol. 1, *God & History.* Downers Grove, IL: InterVarsity Press, 1981.

Bonhoeffer, Dietrich. *Ethics.* New York: Macmillan Publishing Co., 1955.

Bosworth, F. F. *Christ the Healer.* 7th ed. Miami Beach: F. F. Bosworth, 1948.

———. "Do All Speak With Tongues? An open letter to ministers and saints of the Pentecostal movement." Grove City Alliance Church, Grove City, Pennsylvania. http://www.grovecityalliance.org/2007/PDF/Bosworth.pdf.

Bosworth, F. F., to J.W. Welch, 24 July 1918, Assemblies of God Archives, Springfield, MO.

Botterweck, G. Johannes, and Hezmer Ringeren. *Theological Dictionary of the Old Testament.* Grand Rapids: Wm. B. Eerdmans Publishing Co., 1974.

Boyd, Frank M. *The Spirit Works Today.* Springfield, MO: Gospel Publishing House, 1970.

Bradfield, Cecil D. *Neo-Pentecostalism: A Sociological Assessment.* Washington D. C.: University Press of America, 1979.

Bresson, Bernard L. *Studies in Ecstasy.* New York: Vantage Press, 1966.

Bright, Bill. "Importance of the Ministry of the Holy Spirit." *Ministries: the Magazine for Christian Leaders,* Fall 1983, 60–63.

Bromiley, Geoffrey W. *Historical Theology: An Introduction.* Grand Rapids: Wm. B. Eerdmans Publishing Co., 1978.

Brown, Dale W. *Flamed by the Spirit.* Elgin, IL: Brethren Press, 1978.

Bruce, F. F. *1 and 2 Corinthians.* New Century Bible Commentary. Grand Rapids: Wm. B. Eerdmans Publishing Co., 1980.

———. *The Spreading Flame: Advance: The Rise and Progress of Christianity from Its First Beginnings to the Conversion of the English.* Grand Rapids: Wm. B. Eerdmans Publishing Co., 1958.

Brumback, Carl. *Like a River.* Springfield, MO: Gospel Publishing House, 1977.

———. *A Sound from Heaven.* Springfield, MO: Gospel Publishing House, 1977.

———.. *What Meaneth This?* Springfield, MO: Gospel Publishing House, 1947.

Bruner, Frederick D. *A Theology of the Holy Spirit.* Grand Rapids: Wm. B. Eerdmans Publishing Co., 1970.

Bultmann, Rudolph. In *Theological Dictionary of the New Testament*. Edited by Gerhard Kittel and Gerhard Friedrich. Translated by Geoffrey W. Bromiley. Vol. 6, edited by Gerhard Friedrich, 174–228. Grand Rapids: Wm. B. Eerdmans Publishing Co., 1976.

Burdick, Donald W. *Tongues, to Speak or Not to Speak*. Chicago: Moody Press, 1969.

Burgess, Stanley M. *The Spirit and the Church: Antiquity*. Peabody, MA: Hendrickson Publishers, 1984.

Burtner, Robert W., and Robert E. Chiles. *John Wesley's Theology*. Nashville: Abingdon, 1982.

Cairns, Earle E. *Christianity through the Centuries*. Grand Rapids: Zondervan, 1954.

Caldwell, William A. *Pentecostal Baptism*. Tulsa: Front Line Evangelism, 1963.

Carlson, G. Raymond. *Spiritual Dynamics*. Springfield, MO: Gospel Publishing House, Radiant Books, 1976.

Carpenter, Edward. *Common Sense about Christian Ethics*. New York: Macmillan Company, 1961.

Carter, Charles W. *The Person and Ministry of the Holy Spirit*. Grand Rapids: Baker Book House, 1974.

Carter, Howard. *The Gifts of the Spirit*. London: Defoe Press, 1946.

Chadwick, Samuel. *The Way to Pentecost*. Berne, Indiana: Light and Hope Publications, 1937.

Christenson, Larry. *A Message to the Charismatic Movement*. Minneapolis: Bethany Fellowship, Dimension Books, 1972.

———. *Speaking in Tongues*. Minneapolis: Bethany Fellowship, Dimension Books, 1968.

Churchill, Robert K. *Glorious is the Baptism of the Spirit*. Nutley, NJ: Presbyterian and Reformed Publishing Co., 1976.

Clarke, W. K. Lowther. *The Ascetic Works of Saint Basil*. London: Society for Promoting Christian Knowledge, 1925.

Clayton, Allen L. "The Significance of William H. Durham for Pentecostal Historiography." *Pneuma*, Fall 1979, 27–42.

Conn, Charles W. *A Balanced Church*. Cleveland, TN: Pathway Press, 1975.

———. *Like a Mighty Army*. Cleveland, TN: Church of God Publishing House, 1955.

———. *Pillars of Pentecost*. Cleveland, TN: Pathway Press, 1956.

Conybeare, Frederick C. "Gift of Tongues." In *Encyclopedia Britannica*, 1911 ed. Online: Love ToKnow, "Classic Encyclopedia." http://www.1911encyclopedia.org/Gift_Of_Tongues. No pages.

Courtney, Howard P. *The Vocal Gifts of the Spirit*. Los Angeles: H. P. Courtney, 1956.

Cross, James. *A Study of the Holy Ghost*. Cleveland, TN: Pathway Press, 1973.

Culpepper, Robert H. *Evaluating the Charismatic Movement*. Valley Forge, PA: Judson Press, 1977.

Cummings, Robert W. *Unto You Is the Promise*. Springfield, MO: Gospel Publishing House, 1948.

Custance, Arthur C. *Hidden Things of God's Revelation*. The Doorway Papers. Grand Rapids: Zondervan, 1977.

Cutten, George B. *Speaking with Tongues, Historically and Psychologically Considered*. Yale University Press, 1927.

Dalton, Robert Chandler. *Tongues Like as Fire*. Springfield, MO: Gospel Publishing House, 1945.

Damboriena, Prudencio. *Tongues as of Fire*. Washington: Corpus Books, 1969.

Davies, W. D. *Paul and Rabbinic Judaism: Some Rabbinic Elements in Pauline Theology.* Philadelphia: Fortress Press, 1980.

Dayton, Donald W. "The Doctrine of the Baptism of the Holy Spirit: Its Emergence and Significance." *Wesleyan Theological Journal,* Spring 1978, 114–26.

Demarest, Bruce A. *General Revelation.* Grand Rapids: Zondervan, 1982.

Dixon, A. C. *Speaking with Tongues.* Chicago: Bible Institute Colportage Association, n.d.

Dowie, John Alexander. *The Sermons of John Alexander Dowie: Champion of the Faith.* Edited by Gordon Lindsay. Shreveport, LA: The Voice of Healing Publishing Co., n.d.

Drescher, John M. *Spirit Fruit.* Scottdale, PA: Herald Press, 1974.

Drummond, Andrew Landale. *Edward Irving and His Circle, Including Some Consideration of the 'Tongues' Movement in the Light of Modern Psychology.* London: J. Clarke & Co., 1937.

Duncan, George B. *The Person and Work of the Holy Spirit in the Life of the Believer.* Atlanta: John Knox Press, 1973.

Dunn, James D. G. *Baptism in the Holy Spirit.* Philadelphia: Westminster Press, 1970.

———. *Jesus and the Spirit.* Philadelphia: Westminster Press, 1975.

Dunnette, Walter M. *The Interpretation of Holy Scripture: Issues, Principles, Models: An Introduction to Hermeneutics.* Nashville: Thomas Nelson, 1984.

Ellis, E. Earle. *Prophecy and Hermeneutics in Early Christianity.* Grand Rapids: Wm. B. Eerdmans Publishing Co., 1978.

Ellul, Jacques. *The Ethics of Freedom.* Grand Rapids: Wm. B. Eerdmans Publishing Co., 1976.

———. *False Presence of the Kingdom.* New York: Seabury Press, 1972.

———. *The Presence of the Kingdom.* New York: Seabury Press, 1967.

Epp, Theodore H. *The Holy Spirit and the Believer.* Lincoln, NE: Back to the Bible, 1954–79.

———. *The Other Comforter.* Lincoln, NE: Back to the Bible, 1966.

Ervin, Howard M. *Conversion-Initiation and the Baptism in the Holy Spirit.* Peabody, MA: Hendrickson Publishers, 1984.

———. *These Are Not Drunken as Ye Suppose.* Plainfield, NJ: Logos International, 1968.

Evans, Don. "The Spiritual Man." Lecture, 1983 Thomas F. Staley Foundation Lecture Series, Lee University, Cleveland, TN, March 13, 1983.

Ewald, Tod W. "Aspects of Tongues." *The Living Church,* 2 June 1963, 12–13, 19.

Ewert, David. *The Holy Spirit in the New Testament.* Scottdale, PA: Herald Press, 1983.

Farrar, Frederick W. *History of Interpretation.* New York: E. P. Dutton, 1886. Reprint, Grand Rapids: Baker Book House, 1966.

Faupel, David. *The American Pentecostal Movement.* Franklin Springs, GA: The Society for Pentecostal Studies, 1972.

Fee, Gordon D. *New Testament Exegesis.* Philadelphia: Westminster Press, 1983.

———. "Tongues—Least of the Gifts: Some Exegetical Observations on 1 Corinthians 12–14." *Pneuma,* Fall 1980, 3–14.

Fee, Gordon D., and Douglas Stuart. *How to Read the Bible for All Its Worth.* Grand Rapids: Zondervan, Academie Books, 1982.

Floris, Andrew T. "The Charismata in the Post-Apostolic Church." *Paraclete,* Fall 1969, 8–13.

———. "Spiritual Gifts and Macarius of Egypt." *Paraclete,* Summer 1969: 18–20.

Fontenrose, Joseph. *The Delphic Oracle, Its Response and Operations*. Berkeley: University of California Press, 1978.

Foster, K. Neil. *Help! I Believe in Tongues*. Minneapolis: Bethany Fellowship, 1975.

Frend, W. H. C. *The Rise of Christianity*. Philadelphia: Fortress Press, 1984.

Froehlich, Karlfied. *Biblical Interpretation in the Early Church*. Philadelphia: Fortress Press, 1984.

Frost, Robert C. *Aglow with the Spirit*. Northridge, CA: Voice Christian Publications, 1965.

———. *Overflowing Life*. Plainfield, NJ: Logos International, 1971.

Gause, R. Hollis. *Living in the Spirit: The Way of Salvation*. Cleveland, TN: Pathway Press, 1980.

Gee Donald. *Concerning Spiritual Gifts*, rev. ed. Springfield, MO: Gospel Publishing House, 1972.

———. *The Fruit of the Spirit*. Springfield, MO: Gospel Publishing House, 1934.

———. *Spiritual Gifts in the Work of the Ministry*. Los Angeles: L.I.F.E Bible College Alumni Association, 1963.

Geisler, Norman L. *Ethics: Alternatives and Issues*. Grand Rapids: Zondervan, 1971.

Gelpi, Donald L. *Pentecostalism*. New York: Paulist Press, 1971.

General Council of the Assemblies of God. "Minutes of the General Council of the Assemblies of God, 1916." St. Louis, MO, October 2–7, 1916.

Gillquist, Peter. *Let's Quit Fighting about the Holy Spirit*. Grand Rapids: Zondervan, 1974.

Glover, T. R. *Springs of Hellas, and Other Essays by T. R. Glover, with a Memoir by S. C. Roberts*. Cambridge: University Press, 1945. Reprint, New York: Macmillan Co., 1946.

Glueck, Nelson. *Hesed in the Bible*. Translated by Alfred Gottschalk. Cincinnati: Hebrew Union College Press, 1967. Reprint, n.p.: KTAV Publishing House, 1975.

Goodman, Felicitas D. *Speaking in Tongues; a Cross-Cultural Study of Glossolalia*. Chicago: University of Chicago Press, 1972.

Gopplet, Leonhard. *Apostolic and Post-Apostolic Times*. New York: Harper & Row, Harper Torchbooks, 1970.

Gordon, A. J. *The Ministry of the Spirit*. Philadelphia: American Baptist Publication Society, 1894.

Green, Michael. *I Believe in the Holy Spirit*. London: Hodder and Stoughton, 1975. Reprint, Grand Rapids: Wm. B. Eerdmans Publishing Co., 1980.

Griffiths, Michael. *Three Men Filled with the Spirit*. London: Overseas Missionary Fellowship, 1970.

Gromacki, Robert G. *The Modern Tongues Movement*. Philadelphia: Presbyterian and Reformed Publishing Co., 1967.

Gunkel, Hermann. *The Influence of the Holy Spirit*. Philadelphia: Fortress Press, 1979.

Gustafson, James M. *Protestant and Roman Catholic Ethics*. Chicago: University of Chicago Press, 1978.

Hagin, Kenneth E. *Why Every Believer Should Speak in Tongues*. Tulsa: K. E. Hagin, n.d.

Hallett, Garth L. *Christian Moral Reasoning: An Analytic Guide*. Notre Dame: University of Notre Dame Press, 1983.

Harris, R. Laird, et al., eds. *Theological Wordbook of the Old Testament*. Chicago: Moody Press, 1980.

Harris, Ralph W. *Spoken by the Spirit*. Springfield, MO: Gospel Publishing House, 1973.

Harper, Michael. *Live by the Spirit*. Ann Arbor, MI: Servant Books, 1979.

———. *The Love Affair*. Grand Rapids: Wm. B. Eerdmans Publishing Co., 1982.

Haughey, John C. *The Conspiracy of God: The Holy Spirit in Men*. Garden City, NY: Doubleday, 1973.

Hebblethwaite, Brian. *Christian Ethics in the Modern Age*. Philadelphia: Westminster Press, 1982.

Hengel, Martin. *Acts and the History of Earliest Christianity*. Stuttgart: Calwer Verlag, 1979. Reprint, Philadelphia: Fortress Press, 1980.

Henry Carl F. H., ed. *Fundamentals of the Faith*. Grand Rapids: Baker Book House, 1975.

Herbert, Gabriel. *Fundamentalism and the Church*. Philadelphia: Westminster Press, 1957

Heron, Alasdair I. C.. *The Holy Spirit*. Philadelphia: Westminster Press, 1983.

Hertwick, Galen F. "Tongues: An Ecstatic Experience?" *Paraclete,* Fall 1981, 18–20.

Heyer, Robert. *Pentecostal Catholics*. New York: Paulist Press, 1974.

Hillis, Don W. *Tongues, Healing, and You*. Grand Rapids: Baker Book House, 1969.

Hodges, Melvin L. "The Baptism in the Holy Spirit Identified." *Paraclete,* Fall 1971, 22–26.

Hoekema, Anthony A. *Holy Spirit Baptism*. Grand Rapids: Wm. B. Eerdmans Publishing Co., 1972.

———. *What about Tongue-Speaking?* Grand Rapids: Wm. B. Eerdmans Publishing Co., 1966.

Holdcroft, L. Thomas. *The Holy Spirit & Pentecostal Interpretation*. Springfield, MO: Gospel Publishing House, 1962–79.

———. "Spiritual Gifts We May Fail to Recognize." *Paraclete,* Spring 1969, 18–22.

———. "Tongues and the Interpretation of Tongues." *Paraclete,* Summer 1983, 7–12.

Hollenweger, Walter J. "After Twenty Years Research on Pentecostalism." *International Review of Mission* 75 (January 1986): 3–12.

———. *The Pentecostals*. Minneapolis: Augsburg Publishing House, 1972.

Horton, Harold. *The Gifts of the Spirit*. Nottingham, England: Assemblies God Publishing House, 1934. Reprint, Springfield, MO: Gospel Publishing House, 1975.

Horton, Stanley M. *What the Bible Says about the Holy Spirit*. Springfield, MO: Gospel Publishing House, 1976.

Horton, Wade H. *The Glossolalia Phenomenon*. Cleveland, TN: Pathway Press, 1966.

Hosmer, Rachel, and Alan Jones. *Living in the Spirit*. New York: Seabury Press, 1979.

House, H. Wayne. "Tongues and the Mystery Religions of Corinth." *Bibliotheca Sacra,* April–June 1983, 134–38.

Howard, David M. *By the Power of the Holy Spirit*. Downers Grove, IL: InterVarsity Press, 1973.

Hoy, Albert L. "Public and Private Uses of the Gift of Tongues." *Paraclete,* Fall 1968, 10–14.

Hoyle, Peter. *Delphi*. London: Cassell & Co., 1967.

Hunter, Harold D. *Spirit-Baptism: A Pentecostal Alternative*. Lanham, MD: University Press of America, 1983.

———. "Tongues-Speech: A Patristic Analysis." *Journal of the Evangelical Theological Society,* June 1980, 125–33.

Hyde, Walter W. *Paganism to Christianity in the Roman Empire*. New York: Octagon Books, 1970.

Irving, Edward. *Christ's Holiness in Flesh, the Form, Fountain Head, and Assurance to Us of Holiness in Flesh: In Three Parts*. Edinburgh: J. Lindsay, 1831.

James, Maynard. *I Believe in the Holy Ghost*. Minneapolis: Bethany Fellowship, 1965.

Jarman, Ray C. *The Grace and the Glory of God*. Plainfield, NJ: Logos International, 1971.

Jepson, J. W. *What You Should Know about the Holy Spirit.* Van Nuys, CA: Bible Voice Books, 1975.

Jeremias, Joachim. *New Testament Theology.* New York: Charles Scribner's Sons, 1971.

Johnson, Cedric B. *The Psychology of Biblical Interpretation.* Grand Rapids: Zondervan, 1983.

Johnston, Robert K. "Pentecostalism and Theological Hermeneutics: Evangelical Options." *Pneuma,* Spring 1984, 51–66.

Jones, James W. *Filled with New Wine.* San Francisco: Harper & Row, 1974.

Jorstad, Erling. *The Holy Spirit in Today's Church.* Nashville: Abingdon, 1973.

Juel, Donald. *An Introduction to New Testament Literature.* Nashville: Abingdon, 1978.

Kelsey, Morton T. *Encounter with God; a Theology of Christian Experience.* Minneapolis: Bethany Fellowship, 1972.

———. *Tongue Speaking.* Garden City, NY: Doubleday, 1964.

Kennedy, H. A. *St. Paul and the Mystery Religions.* London: Hodder and Stoughton, 1913.

Kenney, Kathleen. "Koinonia as Spirituality." *Quarterly Review,* Summer 1985, 36–43.

Kildahl, John P. *The Psychology of Speaking in Tongues.* New York: Harper & Row, 1972.

Kittel, Gerhard, and Gerhard Friedrich, eds. *Theological Dictionary of the New Testament.* 10 vols. Translated by Geoffrey W. Bromiley. Grand Rapids: Wm. B. Eerdmans Publishing Co., 1976.

Koenig, John. *Charismata: God's Gifts for God's People.* Philadelphia: Westminster Press, 1978.

Kruse, Colin. *New Testament Models for Ministry: Jesus and Paul.* Nashville: Thomas Nelson, 1983.

Kung, Hans, and Jurgen Moltmann. *Conflicts about the Holy Spirit.* New York: Seabury Press, 1979.

Kuyper, Abraham. *Principles of Sacred Theology.* Translated by J. Hendrick De Vries. 1898. Reprint, Grand Rapids: Baker Book House, 1980.

Kydd, Ronald A. N. *Charismatic Gifts in the Early Church.* Peabody, MA: Hendrickson Publishers, 1984.

Ladd, George Eldon. *The Presence of the Future.* Grand Rapids: Wm. B. Eerdmans Publishing Co., 1974.

Laurentin, Rene. *Catholic Pentecostalism.* Garden City, NY: Doubleday & Company, 1977.

LaSor, William S. *The Dead Sea Scrolls and the New Testament.* Grand Rapids: Wm. B. Eerdmans Publishing Co., 1972.

Lemons, Frank W. *Our Pentecostal Heritage.* Cleveland, TN: Pathway Press, 1963.

Lewis, C. S. *The Four Loves.* New York: Harcourt Brace Jovanovich, 1960.

Lightfoot, J. B., ed. *The Apostolic Fathers.* London: Macmillan and Company, 1891. Reprint, Grand Rapids: Baker Book House, 1956–71.

Lillie, D. G. *Tongues under Fire.* Plainfield, NJ: Logos Books, 1966.

Lindblad, Frank. *The Spirit Which Is from God.* Springfield, MO: Gospel Publishing House, 1928.

Lindsell, Harold. *The Holy Spirit in the Latter Days.* Nashville: Thomas Nelson Publishers, 1983.

Long, Edward Leroy, Jr. *A Survey of Christian Ethics.* New York: Oxford University Press, 1967.

Lovelace, Richard F. *Dynamics of Spiritual Renewal.* Downers Grove, IL: InterVarsity Press, 1979.

Lutzer, Erwin. *The Necessity of Ethical Absolutes*. Grand Rapids: Zondervan, Probe Ministries International, 1981.

MacDonald, William. "Pentecostal Theology: A Classical Viewpoint." In *Perspectives on the New Pentecostalism*. Edited by Russell P. Spittler et al., 59–73. Grand Rapids: Baker Book House, 1976.

MacGregor, Geddes. *He Who Lets Us Be: A Theology of Love*. New York: Seabury Press, 1975.

Machen, J. Gresham. *The Origin of Paul's Religion*. Grand Rapids: Wm. B. Eerdmans Publishing Co., 1976.

MacNeil, John. *The Spirit Filled Life*. New York: Fleming H. Revell, 1896. Reprint, Grand Rapids: Baker Book House, 1982.

Maier, John, and Vincent Tollers. *The Bible in Its Literary Milieu*. Grand Rapids: Wm. B. Eerdmans Publishing Co., 1979.

Mallone, George. *Those Controversial Gifts*. Downers Grove, IL: InterVarsity Press, 1983.

Malony, H. Newton. "Debunking Some of the Myths About Glossolalia." *Journal of the American Scientific Affiliation*, 34 (September 1982): 144–48.

Marshall, I. Howard. *Biblical Inspiration*. Grand Rapids: Wm. B. Eerdmans Publishing Co., 1982.

Martin, Ralph P. *The Spirit and the Congregation*. Grand Rapids: Wm. B. Eerdmans Publishing Co., 1984.

Matson, T. B. *Biblical Ethics*. Waco, TX: Word Books, Publishers, 1967.

McAllister, R. E. *The Manifestations of the Spirit*. Toronto: R.E. McAllister, n.d.

McBride, Alfred. *The Gospel of the Holy Spirit*. New York: Hawthorn Books, 1975.

McClintock, John, and James Strong. "The Gift of Tongues." In *Cyclopaedia of Biblical, Theological, and Ecclesiastical Literature* 10:479–86. New York: Harper and Brothers, 1881. Reprint, Grand Rapids: Baker Book House, 1970.

McClung, Grant. "From Bridges (McGavran, 1955) to Waves (Wagner, 1983): Pentecostalism and the Church Growth Movement." *Pneuma*, Spring 1985, 5–18.

McCrossan, T. J. *Speaking with Other Tongues*. Harrisburg, PA: Christian Alliance Publishing Co., 1927.

McDonnell, Kilian. *Charismatic Renewal and the Churches*. New York: Seabury Press, Crossroad, 1976.

———. *The Holy Spirit and Power*. Garden City, New York: Doubleday and Co., 1975.

McGavran, Donald A. *Understanding Church Growth*. Grand Rapids: Eerdmans, 1970.

McGuire, Meredith B. *Pentecostal Catholics: Power, Charisma, and Order in a Religious Movement*. Philadelphia: Temple University Press, 1982.

McKnight, Edgar V. *What is Form Criticism?* Philadelphia: Fortress Press, 1969.

McLean, Mark D. "Toward a Pentecostal Hermeneutic." *Pneuma*, Fall 1984, 35–56.

McPherson, Aimee Semple. *This Is That*. Los Angeles: Echo Park Evangelistic Assoc., 1923.

McQuilkin, J. Robertson. "Limits of Cultural Interpretation." *Journal of the Evangelical Theological Society*, June 1981, 113–24.

Menzies, William W. *Anointed to Serve*. Springfield, MO: Gospel Publishing House, 1971.

Metzger, Bruce M. *The Apocrypha*. New York: Oxford University Press, 1977.

Meyer, Paul W. "The Holy Spirit in the Pauline Letters." *Interpretation*, January 1979, 3–18.

Mickelsen, A. Berkeley. *Interpreting the Bible*. Grand Rapids: Wm. B. Eerdmans Publishing Co., 1963.

Mickelsen, A. Berkeley, and Alvera M. Mickelsen. *Understanding Scripture.* Ventura, CA: Regal Books, 1982.

Miller, Elmer C. *Pentecost Examined by a Baptist Lawyer.* Springfield, MO: Gospel Publishing House, 1936.

Millikin, Jimmy A. *Testing Tongues by the Word.* Nashville: Broadman Press, 1973.

Mills, Watson E. *Speaking in Tongues: A Classified Bibliography.* Franklin Springs, GA: Society for Pentecostal Studies, 1974.

———. *Speaking in Tongues; Let's Talk about It.* Waco, TX: Word Books, Publisher, 1973.

———. *A Theological and Exegetical Approach to Glossolalia.* Lanham, MD: University of America Press, 1985.

———. *Understanding Speaking in Tongues.* Grand Rapids: Wm. B. Eerdmans Publishing Co., 1972.

Mitchell, Charles Buell. *The Theological Seminary of the University of Dubuque Presents the Installation Address ... Entitled "The Place of Church History": Westminster Presbyterian Church, Dubuque, Iowa, May 1, 1963.* 1963.

Mitchell, Robert B. *Heritage & Horizons.* Des Moines: Open Bible Publishers, 1982.

Mohrman, Dick. *Let it Show!* Chappaqua, NY: Christian Herald Books, 1979.

Morris, Leon. *The Gospel According to John.* The New International Commentary on the New Testament. Grand Rapids: Eerdmans, 1971.

———. *I Believe in Revelation.* Grand Rapids: Wm. B. Eerdmans Publishing Co., 1976.

———. *Testaments of Love.* Grand Rapids: Wm. B. Eerdmans Publishing Co., 1981.

Moltmann, Jurgen. *The Church in the Power of the Spirit.* San Francisco: Harper & Row, 1977.

Montague, George T. "Baptism in the Spirit and Speaking in Tongues: A Biblical Appraisal." *Theology Digest* 21 (1973): 342–60.

———. *The Holy Spirit: Growth of a Biblical Tradition.* New York: Paulist Press, 1976.

Montgomery, James A. "Hebrew Hesed and Greek Charis." *Harvard Theological Review,* 32 (April 1959): 97–102.

Morgan, G. Campbell. *The Spirit of God.* New York: Fleming H. Revell Co., 1900.

Moule, C. F. D. *The Holy Spirit.* Grand Rapids: Wm. B. Eerdmans Publishing Co., 1978.

Murray, Andrew. *Full Blessing of Pentecost.* London: Oliphants, 1954.

Nash, Ronald H. *Christian Faith & Historical Understanding.* Grand Rapids: Zondervan / Probe Ministries, 1984.

Nee, Watchman. *The Latent Power of the Soul.* New York: Christian Fellowship Publishers, 1972.

———. *Spiritual Reality or Obsession.* New York: Christian Fellowship Publishers, 1970.

Nelson, Peter Christopher. *Bible Doctrines.* Springfield, MO: Gospel Publishing House, 1948.

Ness, Henry H. *Dunamis and the Church.* Springfield, MO: Gospel Publishing House, 1968.

Nestler, Eric. "Was Montanism a Heresy?" *Pneuma,* Spring 1984, 67–78.

Nichol, John T. *The Pentecostals.* Plainfield, NJ: Logos International, 1966.

Nichols, David R. "The Search for a Pentecostal Structure in Systematic Theology." *Pneuma,* Fall 1984, 57–76.

Nygren, Anders. *Agape & Eros.* Translated by Philip S. Watson. Philadelphia: Westminster Press, 1953. Reprint, Chicago: University of Chicago Press, 1982.

Oliphant, Mrs. (Margaret). *The life of Edward Irving, Minister of the National Scotch Church, London.* New York: Harper & Brothers, 1862.

Osborn, T. L. *The Purpose of Pentecost*. Tulsa: Osborn Foundation International, 1963.

Pache, Rene. *The Person and Work of the Holy Spirit*. Chicago: Moody Press, 1954.

Pamphilus, Eusebius. *The Ecclesiastical History: With an English Translation*. 2 vols. Translated by Kirsopp Lake, J. E. L. Oulton, and H. J. Lawlor. London: W. Heinemann, 1926–1932.

Parham, Sarah E. *Charles F. Parham*. Joplin, MO: Tri-State Printing Co., 1930.

Paris, Arthur E. *Black Pentecostalism: Southern Religion in an Urban World*. Amherst, MA: University of Massachusetts Press, 1982.

Parke, H. W., and D. E. W. Wormell. *The Delphic Oracle*. 2 vols. Oxford: Basil Blackwell, 1956.

Pearlman, Myer. *The Heavenly Gift*. Springfield, MO: Gospel Publishing House, 1935.

———. *Knowing the Doctrines of the Bible*. Springfield, MO: Gospel Publishing House, 1937.

Peck, John. *What the Bible Teaches about the Holy Spirit*. Wheaton, IL: Tyndale House Publishers, 1979.

Perrin, Norman. *What is Redaction Criticism*? Philadelphia: Fortress Press, 1969.

Pinnock, Clark. *The Scripture Principle*. San Francisco: Harper & Row, 1984.

Pinnock, Clark H., and Grant R. Osborne. "A Truce Proposal for the Tongues Controversy." *Christianity Today,* 8 October 1971, 6–9.

Poloma, Margaret. *The Charismatic Movement: Is There a New Pentecost?* Boston: Twayne Publishers, 1982.

Poulsen, Frederik. *Delphi*. London: Gyldendal, 1920.

Preisker, Herbert. "Mainesthai." In *Theological Dictionary of the New Testament*. Edited by Gerhard Kittel and Gerhard Friedrich. Translated by Geoffrey W. Bromiley. Vol. 4, edited by Gerhard Kittel, 360–61. Grand Rapids: Wm. B. Eerdmans Publishing Co., 1976.

Pulkingham, W. Graham. *Gathered for Power*. New York: Morehouse-Barlow Co., 1972.

Qualben, Lars P. *A History of the Christian Church*. New York: Thomas Nelson and Sons, 1958.

Quasten, Johannes, et al., eds. *Ancient Christian Writers*. Vol. 6, *The Didache, The Epistle of Barnabas; The Epistles and the Martyrdom of St. Polycarp; The Fragments of Papias; The Epistle to Diognetus,* edited by Johannes Quasten and Joseph C. Plumpe. New York: Newman Press, 1948.

Quebedeaux, Richard. *The New Charismatics*. Garden City, NY: Doubleday & Co., 1976.

Rahner, Karl. *The Spirit in the Church*. New York: Seabury Press, Crossroad, 1979.

Ramm, Bernard. *After Fundamentalism*. San Francisco: Harper & Row, 1983.

———. *Hermeneutics*. Grand Rapids: Baker Book House, 1967.

———. *Protestant Biblical Interpretation*. Boston: W. A. Wilde Co., 1956.

———. *The Right, the Good and the Happy*. Waco, TX: Word Books, 1971.

———. *Special Revelation and the Word of God*. Grand Rapids: Wm. B. Eerdmans Publishing Co., 1961.

Ramsey, Michael. *Holy Spirit*. Grand Rapids: Wm. B. Eerdmans Publishing Co., 1977.

Ramsey, Michael, and Leon-Joseph Suenens. *Come Holy Spirit*. New York: Morehouse-Barlow Co., 1976.

Ranaghan, Kevin, and Ranaghan, Dorothy. *Catholic Pentecostals*. New York: Paulist Press, 1969.

Rea, John, ed. *The Layman's Commentary on the Holy Spirit*. Plainfield, NJ: Logos International, 1974.

Reid, Tommy. *The Exploding Church.* Plainfield, NJ: Logos International, 1979.

Rengstorf, Karl. "Semeion." In *Theological Dictionary of the New Testament.* Edited by Gerhard Kittel and Gerhard Friedrich. Translated by Geoffrey W. Bromiley. Vol. 7, edited by Gerhard Friedrich, 200–61. Grand Rapids: Wm. B. Eerdmans Publishing Co., 1976.

Roberts, Oral. *The Baptism with the Holy Spirit and the Value of Speaking in Tongues Today.* Tulsa, OK: O. Roberts, 1964.

Roebling, Karl. *Pentecostals around the World.* Hicksville, NY: Exposition Press, 1978.

Rubenstein, Richard L. *The Cunning of History.* New York: Harper & Row, Publishers, Colophon Books, 1975.

Ruef, John. *Paul's First Letter to Corinth,* Philadelphia: Westminster Press, 1977.

Rusch, William G. "The Doctrine of the Holy Spirit in the Patristic and Medieval Church." In *The Holy Spirit in the Life of the Church: From Biblical Times to the Present.* Edited by Paul D. Opsahl, 66–98. Minneapolis: Augsburg Publishing House, 1978.

Ruthven, Jon. "The Cessation of the Charismata, Part One: A Survey of a Prevailing Viewpoint." *Paraclete,* Spring 1969, 23–30.

———. "The Cessation of the Charismata, Part Two: An Evaluation of Some Popular Presuppositions." *Paraclete,* Summer 1969, 21–27.

———. "The Cessation of the Charismata, Part Three: A Biblical Defense for Continuation of the Charismata." *Paraclete,* Fall 1969, 20–28.

———. "Is Glossolalia Languages?" *Paraclete,* Spring 1968, 27–30.

Ryrie, Charles C. *The Holy Spirit.* Chicago: Moody Press, 1965.

Samarin, William J. *Tongues of Men and Angels.* New York: Macmillan, 1972.

Sanders, E. P., ed. *Jewish and Christian Self-Definition,* Vol. 1, *The Shaping of Christianity in the Second and Third Centuries.* Philadelphia: Fortress Press, 1980.

Sanders, J. Oswald. *The Holy Spirit and His Gifts.* J. O. Sanders, 1940. Reprint, Grand Rapids: Zondervan, 1970.

Savelle, Jerry. *The Spirit of Might.* Tulsa: Harrison House, 1982.

Schweizer, Eduard. *The Holy Spirit.* Translated by Reginald H. and Ilse Fuller. Stuttgart: Kreu Verlag, 1978; Philadelphia: Fortress Press, 1980.

Sheppard, Gerald T. "Pentecostalism and the Hermeneutics of Dispensationalism: Anatomy of an Uneasy Relationship." *Pneuma,* Fall 1984, 5–33.

Sherrill, John L., and Elizabeth Sherrill. *They Speak with Other Tongues.* Westwood, NJ: Spire Books, 1964.

Sims, John A. *Power with Purpose.* Cleveland, TN: Pathway Press, 1984.

Singer, Irving. *The Nature of Love; Plato to Luther.* New York: Random House Books, 1966.

Smail, Thomas A. *Reflected Glory.* Grand Rapids: Wm. B. Eerdmans Publishing Co., 1975.

Smeeton, Donald Dean. "The Charismatic Theology of R. A. Torrey." *Paraclete* , Fall 1980, 20–23.

Sorg, Rembert James. *Hesed and Hasid in the Psalms.* Vol. 2, God's Love Songs Series. St. Louis: Pio Decimo Press, 1953.

Southey, Robert. *The Book of the Church.* London: Frederick Warne and Co., 1869.

Sparks, Jack N., ed. *The Apostolic Fathers.* Nashville: Thomas Nelson Publishers, 1978.

Spittler, Russell P., ed. *Perspectives on the New Pentecostalism.* Grand Rapids: Baker Book House, 1976.

Sproul, R. C. *Knowing Scripture.* Downers Grove, IL: InterVarsity Press, 1977.

Stiles, J. E. *The Gift of the Holy Spirit.* Burbank, CA: J. E. Stiles, n.d.

Stott, John R. W. *Baptism & Fullness.* Leicester, England: Tyndale Press, 1964. Reprint, Downers Grove, IL: InterVarsity Press, 1976.

———. *God's Book for God's People.* Downers Grove, IL: InterVarsity Press, 1982.

Strachan, Gordon. *The Pentecostal Theology of Edward Irving.* London: Darton, Longman and Todd, 1973.

Stronstad, Roger. *The Charismatic Theology of St. Luke.* Peabody, MA: Hendrickson Publishers, 1984.

Stuhlmacher, Peter. *Historical Criticism and Theological Interpretation of Scripture.* Philadelphia: Fortress Press, 1977.

Swete, Henry B. *The Holy Spirit in the New Testament.* Grand Rapids: Baker Book House, 1964.

Synan, Vinson. *Aspects of Pentecostal-Charismatic Origins.* Plainfield, NJ: Logos International, 1975.

———. *The Holiness-Pentecostal Movement in the United States.* Grand Rapids: Wm. B. Eerdmans Publishing Co., 1971.

Tanneberg, Ward M. *Let Light Shine Out.* Walnut Creek, CA: Moore, Mayhew and Fick, 1977.

Tatham, C. Ernest. *Let the Tide Come In!* Carol Stream, IL: Creation House, 1976.

Tertullian and Peter Holmes. *The Five Books against Marcion.* Vol. 7, Ante-Nicene Christian Library. Edinburgh: T. & T. Clark, 1878.

Thieleke, Helmut. *The Evangelical Faith.* 3 vols. Grand Rapids: Wm. B. Eerdmans Publishing Co., 1974–82.

———. *Theological Ethics.* Vol. 1, *Foundations,* edited by William H. Lazareth. Philadelphia: Fortress Press, 1966.

———. *Theological Ethics.* Vol. 3, *Sex,* edited by William H. Lazareth. Translated by John W. Doberstein. Grand Rapids: Baker Book House, 1975. Reprint, Grand Rapids: Wm. B. Eerdmans Publishing Co., 1979.

Thiselton, Anthon C. *The Two Horizons: New Testament Hermeneutics and Philosophical Description.* Grand Rapids: Wm. B. Eerdmans Publishing Co., 1980.

Thomas, Robert L. *Understanding Spiritual Gifts.* Chicago: Moody Press, 1978.

Torrance, Thomas F. *Reality and Evangelical Theology: The Realism of Christian Revelation.* Philadelphia: Westminster Press, 1982. Reprint, Downer's Grove, IL: InterVarsity Press, 1999.

Torrey, R. A. *The Baptism with the Holy Spirit.* Minneapolis: Bethany Fellowship, Dimension Books, 1972.

———. *How to Obtain Fullness of Power.* New York: Fleming H. Revell Co., 1897.

———. *The Person and Work of the Holy Spirit,* rev. ed. Grand Rapids: Zondervan, 1974.

Traina, Robert. *A Methodical Bible Study.* Grand Rapids: Zondervan, Francis Asbury Press, 1980.

Unger, Merrill F. *New Testament Teachings on Tongues.* Grand Rapids: Kregel Publications, 1971.

Unger, Merrill F., and William White, eds. *Nelson's Expository Dictionary of the Old Testament.* Nashville: Thomas Nelson, 1980.

Verhey, Allen. *The Great Reversal: Ethics and the New Testament.* Grand Rapids: Wm. B. Eerdmans Publishing Co., 1984.

Versteeg, John M. *Perpetuating Pentecost.* New York: Willet, Clark & Colby, 1930.

Waddams, Herbert. *A New Introduction to Moral Theology.* New York: Seabury Press, 1964.

Wagner, C. Peter. *Our Kind of People: The Ethical Dimension of Church Growth in America.* Atlanta: John Knox Press, 1979.

———. "What About Tongues Speaking?" *Eternity,* March 1968, 24–26.

Walston, Rick. *The Speaking in Tongues Controversy.* Longwood, FL: Xulon Press, 2003.

Walvoord, John F. *The Holy Spirit at Work Today.* Chicago: Moody Press, 1973.

———. *The Holy Spirit.* Grand Rapids: Zondervan, 1976.

Watson, David C. K. *Called & Committed.* Wheaton, IL: Harold Shaw Publishers, 1982.

———. *One in the Spirit.* London: Hodder & Stoughton, 1973. Reprint, Old Tappan, NJ: Fleming H. Revell, 1974.

Wead, R. Douglas. *Father McCarthy Smokes a Pipe and Speaks in Tongues.* Norfolk, VA: Wisdom House Publishing Co., 1972.

White, R. E. O. *The Answer Is the Spirit.* Philadelphia: Westminster Press, 1979.

———. *Biblical Ethics.* Atlanta: John Knox Press, 1979.

Wiebe, Phillip H. "The Pentecostal Initial Evidence Doctrine." *Journal of the Evangelical Theological Society,* December 1984, 465–72.

Williams, Ernest S. *Systematic Theology.* 3 vols. Springfield, MO: Gospel Publishing House, 1953.

Williams, John. *The Holy Spirit, Lord and Life-Giver.* Neptune, NJ: Loizeaux Brothers, 1980.

Williams, J. Rodman. *The Era of the Spirit.* Plainfield, NJ: Logos International, 1971.

———. *The Gift of the Holy Spirit Today.* Plainfield, NJ: Logos International, 1980.

———. *The Pentecostal Reality.* Plainfield, NJ: Logos International, 1972.

Winehouse, Irwin. *The Assemblies of God, a Popular Survey.* New York: Vantage Press, 1959.

Wogen, Norris L. *Jesus, Where Are You Taking Us?* Carol Stream, IL: Creation House, 1973.

Woodworth-Etter, Maria. *Signs & Wonders.* Tulsa: Harrison House, n.d.

Wunderlich, Lorenz. *The Half-Known God.* Saint Louis: Concordia Publishing House, 1963.

Yohn, Rick. *Beyond Spiritual Gifts.* Wheaton; IL: Tyndale House Publishers, 1976.

.

www.ingramcontent.com/pod-product-compliance
Lightning Source LLC
Chambersburg PA
CBHW060342100426
42812CB00003B/1096